DIY Kitchen Chemistry

Simple Homemade Bath & Body Projects

By Kayla Fioravanti, R.A.
Certified and Registered Aromatherapist, Cosmetic Formulator

Other Books by Kayla
The Art, Science and Business of Aromatherapy,
Your Guide for Personal Aromatherapy and Entrepreneurship

How to Make Melt and Pour Soap Base from Scratch,
A Beginner's Guide to Melt and Pour Soap Base Manufacturing

Coming Soon!
When I was Young I Flew the Sun as a Kite

Puffy and Blue

DIY Kitchen Chemistry
Simple Homemade Bath & Body Project

By Kayla Fioravanti, R.A.
Certified and Registered Aromatherapist, Cosmetic Formulator

Editing by Dana Brown

Cover and Text Design by Alex Badcock

Copyright © 2011 by Kayla Fioravanti

ISBN-13: 978-0615580562 (Selah Press)
ISBN-10: 0615580564

Printed in the United States of America

Published by
Selah Press

Dedication

To my children,

Keegan, you were the inspiration on my journey in becoming an accidental aromatherapist.

Selah and Caiden, you are my very favorite Kitchen Chemists.

"Behold, children are a heritage from the Lord, the fruit of the womb a reward."
Psalm 127:3

Acknowledgements

The Kitchen Chemistry TV series on YouTube was the inspiration for this book. I never would have started filming the series without the encouragement of my husband Dennis. His constant leadership is a solid foundation I depend on. Thanks for leading me here, Honey.

The Kitchen Chemistry TV series was made possible by the creative genius of Alex Badcock. His editing, graphics and hard work made me look good. He edited out my "ums" and edited in wonderful flow and cadence for the series. Alex's work on this book, as well as my other books, How to Make Melt & Pour Soap from Scratch and The Art, Science and Business of Aromatherapy has been priceless.

Special thanks to my editor, Dana Brown, for cleaning up my grammar. Thanks for treating this "baby" with your special touch and care.

Being part of the cosmetic industry has been an amazing journey. I have found great friendship and support among my peers, especially Donna Maria Coles Johnson of the Indie Beauty Network. Thank you for always being available on the other side of the phone, email and even on social media channels to me and all the mad kitchen chemists out there. You are a God-send! Long live the Sweaty Beauty Network who pounded the pavement many a summer in the halls of Congress to advocate on behalf of small and independent businesses.

My mother was an incredibly creative woman, and I am so grateful for having lived in her shadow. My mom and dad encouraged and nurtured my inner kitchen chemist, and I will be forever thankful for the honor of having them as parents.

A special shout out to Selah and Caiden who waited so patiently through mom being busy writing three books in nine months.

Most importantly I am eternally grateful for my Lord and Savior, Jesus Christ. "For from him and through him and to him are all things. To him be the glory forever! Amen." Romans 11:36

Table of Contents

About the Author

Kayla is a Certified, ARC Registered Aromatherapist and the co-Founder of Essential Wholesale and its lab division, Essential Labs. She is a wife and mother of three. She started her company along with her husband, Dennis. In 1998, Kayla started creating products in her kitchen using essential oils and a $50 investment. Over the years Dennis and Kayla turned the profit from their first batch of products into more supplies and repeated the process over and over again, remaining a debt free company.

In 2000, Dennis and Kayla started an all-natural aromatherapy based Home Party Plan. In 2002, they changed their business plan and became the distribution and manufacturing company, Essential Wholesale. This was followed by the addition of Essential Labs in 2005. The initial $50 investment from their home kitchen, combined with blood, sweat and prayers, has now become a multi-million dollar organically certified and U.S. Food and Drug Administration (FDA) compliant company.

Kayla has passionately shared her knowledge of aromatherapy, crafting, business, and formulating. She is the go-to industry specialist for formulating aromatherapy, natural, organic and pure cosmetics and personal care items. She has formulated thousands of products including: mineral make up, skin care, body care, and products for bath, spa, hair, baby, pets, aroma and much more. Through her lab division, Essential Labs, Kayla has formulated private-label personal care products for hundreds of businesses worldwide.

Kayla can be found on YouTube where she teaches a variety of do-it-yourself (DIY) recipes for the Essential Wholesale series called "Kitchen Chemistry TV." Kayla's articles can be found in dozens of publications including: Dermascope Magazine, Les Nouvelles Esthetique, Global Cosmetic Industry (GCI) Magazine, New York Metro Parent, Saponifier, National Association of Holistic Aromatherapy and Essential Wholesale's educational arm, the Essential U blog. Kayla has been featured in, and has given expert advice to hundreds of magazines including: Real Simple, Self Magazine, Prevention Magazine, Good Housekeeping, Home Business Magazine, Women Entrepreneur, Elle, Private Label Buyer, Redbook, InStyle Magazine, Woman's World and more.

Kayla wrote a chapter in the book *Millionaire Mom: The Art of Raising a Business and a Family at the Same Time* by Joyce Bone. Her quotes are featured in the 2009 and 2010 "The Woman's Advantage" calendar. Kayla has been a guest on radio programs such as Millionaire Moms Radio, The Organic View, Organic Beauty Radio, Indie Radio, KPDQ Northwest Showcase, Good Day Oregon, 104.1 The Fish, and many others.

Kayla has been an outspoken advocate for small business owners in the halls of Congress since 2007. Kayla created the Essential U blog, an educational center for aromatherapy, cosmetics, industry standards, and business ownership. She has been an expert on the website Personal Care Truth, Information Based on Scientific Facts, because of her passion to spread science-based factual information about cosmetics and the personal care industry. One of her goals is to help protect small businesses from regulatory interference which may hamper the pursuit of the American dream.

Introduction

This book is designed to provide fun bath and body products that you can make in your kitchen for personal use, retail or to give as gifts. It covers equipment, ingredient information and recipes. If you are seeking in depth information on business development, quality control measures, good manufacturing practices, regulations, and/or aromatherapy then I recommend supplementing this book with one or both of my other two books.

The topics covered in depth in each book are:

How to Make Melt and Pour Soap Base from Scratch
- Business Tips
- Equipment Tips
- Ingredient Information
- MSDS Overview
- Lye Handling Safety Tips
- Recipes and Methodology to make M&P Soap base from Scratch
- Basics of Additives, Coloring and Scenting M&P Soap
- FDA on Soap, Cosmetics and Drug
- INCI information
- Good Manufacturing Tips

The Art, Science and Business of Aromatherapy
- An in depth survey of the scientific foundation of aromatherapy
- Essential Oils versus Fragrance Oils
- History of Aromatherapy
- The Psychology and Physiology of Aromatherapy
- Safety Measures and Precautions
- 21 in depth Essential Oil Profiles
- The Art of Blending Essential Oils
- Using Essential Oils in Business and Products
- Skin Care Information
- Business Tips and Advice
- Recipes to Create Bath & Body Products and Soap
- Industry Regulations Information
- Standards and Practices
- Practical Good Manufacturing Practices Tips
- Navigating the FDA and Labeling Rules
- Essential Oil Crop Calendar
- Aromatherapy Schools
- And so much more….

All of the Kitchen Chemistry recipes in this book have a matching Kitchen Chemistry video on YouTube that can be found at *http://www.youtube.com/user/essentialwholesale/videos*

Chapter 1
The Rest of the Business Story

I always liked it when Paul Harvey would say, "…and now you know the rest of the story." Many readers already know the business story of the company I started in my kitchen with my husband from the Essential U blog or my other two books *How to Make Melt & Pour Soap Base from Scratch* and *The Art, Science and Business of Aromatherapy*. For you readers who don't know the story, I am sharing below the well-known portions of our Essential Wholesale journey. And for those who have already read it, I'm filling in the "rest of the story."

In the Beginning, There was Tea Tree

The story of how I got started in the aromatherapy, soap, natural cosmetics and personal care industry is very much like the story of many others who start a small business: I was fulfilling a personal need. It was the summer of 1998 when my son, Keegan, got a case of ringworm on his face that would not go away.

The Rest of the Story…

This infamous case of ringworm showed up right below Keegan's eye just days before Dennis and I were to be married. I normally wouldn't have gotten a doctor involved for what I expected to be a simple case of ringworm, but being a vain bride I wanted his face picture perfect for the wedding photographs. We not only visited the doctor, but we tried a prescription as the first line of defense. When it failed the doctor told me to try an OTC crème. It also failed and Keegan is wearing concealer in our wedding photos.

We tried Over-the-Counter (OTC) drugs and prescriptions to clear it up, but it kept growing. Since I was partly raised while living overseas, I had learned to go to the apothecary to find natural cures. So I headed to the tiny, local health food store where we were living in Edmond, Oklahoma as it was the closest thing I could find to an apothecary. The store clerk had nothing to do but stand in the book aisle and read books with me. Everything we read pointed to tea tree essential oil as the cure to ringworm.

At that time, our family was on a very tight student budget, so I bought the smallest bottle of tea tree essential oil and headed home to see if my eleven-dollar investment would work. Much to my surprise, within three days the ringworm was completely gone. In addition, I had expected the tea tree to cause allergic reactions because I am allergic to fragrances, but I had no problems. Because of that combination of events, I became very intrigued about this thing called aromatherapy.

Before that encounter with tea tree essential oil, I had always just assumed that aromatherapy was one of the foo-foo fluffery esoteric things out there in the market. When I thought of aromatherapy I envisioned the incense burners that make me take the long way around the hippy haven stores that line Hawthorne Avenue in Portland, Oregon.

With my new-found interest in the healing benefits of essential oils, I went to the local library and checked out every book they had on aromatherapy. After I read those, I put in a request for all of the aromatherapy books available in the state to be sent to my local library. Once I started digging into the science of essential oils, I was fully addicted to learning. It was then that I started researching and studying to become a certified aromatherapist.

The Rest of the Story...

During that time there were days I would leave the library with stacks of books taller than my six year old son. And because of a humiliating experience I had as a child, I learned how to ingest large sums of information. In 5th grade I was sent to Special Education because my piano teacher noticed my eyes were not working together. Thankfully she realized I wasn't just a bad piano student, but that I was simply not getting information correctly from my eyes to my brain.

I went to the Special Education Department every week to retrain my eyes. I sat in front of an antiquated machine that rushed words of a story past my eyes. At first it was a gray, blurred line that frustrated me. Eventually it worked and I became a strong reader, something that has served me well in business and life. I never imagined the skills I was learning would make it possible for me to devour the piles of books I read to study aromatherapy and dissect cosmetic formulating. All I could see at the time was my wounded pride and hours of frustrating therapy.

There are moments in life that seem so remedial. We get frustrated with the extra steps we have to take to get to the place others reach in one leap. And yet, as we walk through these moments, we are building the foundation of our own bridge that will lead us to our individual successes. Don't burn that bridge just because the journey was humiliating. There are valuable lessons being learned even when we think life isn't fair.

At that time I was a stay at home mom, homeschooling my now-ringworm-free son, while my husband was a full-time student and working full-time! When Christmas arrived we needed to make our gifts because we couldn't afford to purchase them. So, I decided to use the tea tree from our medicine cabinet to scent the melt and pour soap we bought from the local craft store. We created an assortment of soaps with different sizes and shapes and packaged them up nicely. My husband, Dennis, has a long history of creating companies, so he decided to add re-order forms along with the gifts. In retrospect it might have been a bit tacky, but it worked!

Our friends and family loved the soap and, not only did they order more, but they referred us to their friends and family. When the orders came in we just kept making more, thinking our little hobby would be nothing more than that, but we were wrong! Bit by bit people began asking for more products and we started to expand our line at first by buying from overseas or out of Canada since no one in the U.S. made bulk natural products at the time. We started to realize that our little Oklahoma-based aromatherapy hobby was turning into a miniature micro-business.

The Rest of the Story...
Dennis and I met while working in Amway. So in reality we went from one soap business to another.

When my mother suffered a heart attack, I felt the need to move back to the Northwest to be closer to my parents. But our hobby didn't bring in enough funds to afford us the luxury of moving. It wasn't until shortly after I totaled our car in an accident that an opportunity presented itself. When a $6,000 check came in the mail to replace our car Dennis asked if I would prefer to use it to move to Portland or to buy a new car? I jumped at the opportunity to take the money and move our family and business back to the Pacific Northwest with the car we had left.

It was a Friday, and on the following Monday Dennis was scheduled to start his training with the Police Academy – so it was now or never. So that Monday, instead of it being the first day at the Academy for Dennis, it became moving day. We loaded the back of our U-Haul with all of our earthly garage-sale possessions along with a small box filled with essential oils and soap molds. In the cab of the U-Haul we packed in one car seat with our six week-old baby Selah, one cat litter box, one beloved cat named Star, two adults and our 6 year-old son Keegan.

It was a snug fit, but we were excited. We had just enough money to get us to Portland to set up our new lives. We hitched our 12 year-old car onto the back and headed North to a land of unknowns. We had no job, no place to live, and very limited resources with only 5 days to return the truck before we got charged again…But we were full of hope, aspirations, and dreams. Anything seemed possible.

After about twenty miles, just outside Oklahoma City, the truck broke down for the first time. After a couple of hours of quick repairs, we continued our journey. Everything was going well until the next day. As we drove up a long incline in Burley, Idaho, we noticed lots of black smoke pouring of our U-Haul. This time there were no quick repairs to be made. The U-Haul guys unhooked our car, towed our U-Haul off the highway, and set us free in the Middle-of-Nowhere-Ville, Idaho. We holed up in a seedy hotel with our cat, a baby, and a 6 year-old while repairs were made, and our time and resources diminished. We were detoured, but we were not fazed – yet.

With our truck fixed three days later, the guys at U-Haul hitched our little car back onto the tow dolly and sent us on our way with promises to reimburse us for our detour sometime later. We left Burley with even more dreams. Dennis has spent the down time imagining up new divisions and exciting directions. I have to admit, our little detour sparked new ideas in Dennis' mind that—by the sheer size of those dreams—scared me.

With one day to spare before the U-Haul was due to be returned, we rolled into Portland, Oregon in need of a job and a home. We unhitched our car from the U-Haul and found that it had aspirations of its own: to roll down the hill and away from us undeterred by the constrictions of brakes. We discovered that we had literally dragged our twelve year old Toyota the five hundred and eighty six miles between Burley, Idaho and Portland, Oregon with the emergency brake engaged. The U-Haul mechanic had set it when he loaded our car back on the dolly and forgotten to release it. Still undaunted, we forked over our formally-earmarked house deposit money to have brand new brakes put on our old car. We rented a car so we could still find a place to live that day.

Traditional home rental options were out since we had no deposit funds left, no jobs, no income, no credit, and very little money. Our journey had depleted our funds for first and last month's rent, security deposit, and all the other fees those people threw at us, walking in the door. After several rejections in town, we found ourselves driving way out in to the countryside in the small town of Molalla. As we drove through a cute little neighborhood, Dennis suddenly stopped the car to talk to a man putting up a For Sale sign in the lawn.

A few minutes later, Dennis came back to the car and said, "Let's go get the truck." Despite our situation, he had convinced that man to rent us his home until it sold. He handed him a check for that month's rent and drove back to get all our worldly belongings so that we could move into our cute, new home.

We were ready to unpack and settle in so we could get back to our new hobby business.

However, when we pulled the U-Haul up to the house with great anticipation, and we released the back door of the U-Haul to unpack, we found that all our life possessions and our "business in one box" was covered in thick black soot. It seemed that the black smoke that had poured out of the U-Haul truck had been going directly into the storage area of the truck. We suddenly had no clothes, bedding or furniture—nothing was spared!

A few set-backs later—and even more broke than we had planned—we got ourselves settled into the Northwest. We started homeschooling Keegan, and Dennis started school. Our Molalla home-front meant that Dennis had a 36 mile commute each way to and from school. Between his studies, though, we started building our dreams into a business.

Our kitchen became our R&D lab. I ordered more library books and, in between homeschooling and caring for our little baby, filled my mind with more information on aromatherapy and cosmetics. Business came natural to Dennis, and he began building up our mail-order aromatherapy business as we sat on the floor of our new home with our new particle-board desk furniture. We were not willing to allow the roadblocks, detours, and distractions to stop us from reaching for goals.

The Rest of the Story...

My most vivid memory of this time period is of me spending every one of Selah's naps in the kitchen madly creating and experimenting. I remember producing my very first crème and being so proud despite the fact that it bore a strong resemblance to Crisco shortening. I proudly presented the crème to my mother, who promptly praised it while slathering it onto her skin. I also spent long hours at the downtown Portland library reading and researching. The entire industry was foreign to me and I created an immersion program for myself. We only had one car so my time was dictated by Keegan's boredom, Selah's fussy level and Dennis' school schedule.

A few weeks later a friend noticed how enthusiastic I was about aromatherapy, so she invited me to have a product party at her house and teach what I knew about essential oils. She invited her friends over, and I taught them all about aromatherapy. Two of the women asked how they could become consultants and sell my product. I wrote down their info and promised to get back to them. I went home with $500 worth of orders and a new idea. Dennis took that idea and ran with it. He developed a multi-level business plan and manual. We signed up our first consultants that same week. As we grew our party plan, we endured yet another move to be closer to Dennis' school. Meanwhile we continued to fill the orders for our little multi-level business out of our small apartment kitchenette.

The Rest of the Story…
One of the "benefits" of buying from us at this time was that we delivered all of our products to our customers. We didn't want anyone to see just how small our business was so we offered free delivery anywhere in the Portland metro area. I timed my delivery drop off around Selah's nap times so she could sleep in the car while I drove all over town.

The party plan really took off, and we found ourselves supporting over fifty consultants after only a few months. As we raced around trying to fill orders we realized that we had to move the business out of our two-bedroom apartment kitchenette to a "huge" 600 square-foot building to keep up with our growing need for ingredients and supply space. We were very scared because that was a huge investment for us with absolutely no guarantee of success. I thought, "Well if we fail, at least we can move into our manufacturing space until our lease is up."

In the middle of all of this, our family expanded with the birth of our daughter Caiden, and we were determined to keep everyone with us while we grew our business. Dennis focused on growing the business while I made the products. We were completely overwhelmed as we worked night and day toward a vision that was not very clear at the time and changed often. We contacted all of the cosmetic manufacturing companies in search of someone who would private label for us or custom formulate product that met our needs. It was then that we discovered that the industry purchase minimums were either 4 drums (220 gallons) or 10,000 pieces and we couldn't afford or store either one. With new challenges facing us, Dennis and I decided to re-invent how "natural" cosmetics were being made, so I went back to the library to do more research, and the journey continued.

The Rest of the Story…
While pregnant with Caiden I produced all of our products. I often had one in the belly and one on my back. Selah loved to rule the world from a backpack I wore while working. She would chat and chipper away, while Caiden kicked and bounced in my belly. Since we were homeschooling Keegan at the time, he would sit and do his homework at a table that doubled as a filling line.

> With all of my pregnancies I endured contractions starting in month five. Because I was on my feet so much the contractions were particularly bad with Caiden. I often had to stop what I was doing and lay down in the middle of the manufacturing floor on my left side to slow down the contractions. It was my own version of stop, drop, roll on side and rest.

This was long before there were craft books on how to make bath and body products. I read all of the copyrighted recipes of the chemical companies in order to better understand the chemistry of cosmetics. Once I gathered enough knowledge to understand the concept of emulsion and preservation, I became a research and development queen. I ordered samples of ingredients, and by trial and error I created our own cosmetic formulas that were safe, stable, and made with naturally-derived ingredients.

Once we had perfected our formulas, Dennis realized that there was a giant niche in the industry that was wide open. No one was offering "natural" bulk bases to the small businesses, crafters, or hobby-level consumers. He also determined that it would be much easier to manufacture in bulk and sell to thousands of small businesses than it was to make one retail product at a time.

I was terrified. I knew Dennis would succeed and I couldn't imagine making hundreds if not thousands of gallons-worth of product. I was making all of our products in two-gallon batches! I remember clearly the sheer panic that overtook me when Dennis announced that we were going to change our business model in the midst of our original aromatherapy party plan company. I had worked so many hours writing training material, formulating products, doing parties, training consultants, making product, and doing everything else it took to build our party plan business from scratch. We were busier than you could imagine, growing substantially while working our tails off.

Dennis had this bright idea to start a new company and call it Essential Wholesale. He wanted to shut down the party plan and become a wholesale manufacturer of the cosmetic bases, using the formulas we had developed. It seemed counter intuitive to me to shut down something that, for all intents and purposes, was working. He was totally sold out on his new vision for our future, but I was scared of the change. What I didn't know—but what Dennis could see clearly—was that the party plan business was about to implode because its growth was unsustainable given our lack of capital resources.

The Rest of the Story...

Dennis purchased a $35 program at Office Depot to build the Essential Wholesale website. He had never built or operated a website before, but that didn't deter him from creating a website that made our tiny business look huge. In reality, each day we were buying just enough supplies to fill the orders for the next day. Every day we picked up our supplies, manufactured our products and repackaged our raw materials into smaller quantities to fill orders for that day. By the end of the day we placed our next order, based on that day's orders, to do it all over again. It was labor intensive and insane, but we kept it up until we were able to start buying in larger quantities.

I remember when we first started buying our coconut oil in drums we couldn't afford a drum heater so I had to cut the solid oil out of the drum to manufacture each day. The hard part was when we got about midway into the drum my pregnant belly was a bit awkward to work around.

The reality was that we were working around the clock, and nothing about our business model left an opportunity for that to ever change. Our mistake was that when a customer attended one of our parties they had the ability to order a customized aromatherapy product for their exact needs. That meant that every product had to be scented and mixed by me, because the use of the correct dose of each essential oil in a given product could only be determined by a trained aromatherapist—and I was it. We were working until two or four a.m., only to go back to our office by nine a.m. and do it all again. It was insane, but I was afraid that if we changed I would have to pay the same dues to succeed in the new company.

Dennis had the forethought to change our business model so that someday our jobs would be able to be duplicated. Our organically-grown business that had started with only fifty dollars, combined with a significant investment of time and effort, needed a makeover.

I was emotionally hanging onto all the time and energy we had invested into our party plan. Dennis was using logic and striving for a better future for us. I was frightened of the change. Dennis talked about one day making thousands of gallons of product in one batch, and I wondered how I could physically do that, given that I was killing myself to produce the few gallons we produced per week at that point.

Thankfully I let go of my worries and grasped onto the dreams of my husband. I made the leap with my eyes wide open, hands shaking, heart palpitating, and my vision firmly focused on Dennis' dream. Once I made the successful leap to his dream, it became mine. I thank God that I was able to set aside my fear of change and let go of a faulty future that would have held us back from our greatest potential.

Our original business, FCP Parties, ran from 1999 to 2001. In 2001 we began the early stages of launching Essential Wholesale, and we were exclusively supported by that division by October of 2002. And 2003 was our first year of having only Essential Wholesale sales and customers. So for four years, from 1998 through 2002, we transitioned from one idea to another, blindly weaving our way toward an idea that had yet to be discovered. Finally, in 2003 we embarked on our continuing journey with Essential Wholesale.

We created Essential Wholesale with no minimum dollar amount for bulk wholesale product and 2 gallon minimums for custom formulating. Essential Wholesale hit the ground running. We quickly outgrew our 600 square-foot facility and moved to a 2,500 square foot space. We outgrew that space within five months but still managed to operate there for one and-a-half years.

The Rest of the Story...

During the year and a half that we operated at the 2,500 square foot space we had to crawl over the top of drums to get to the one we needed. Our storage area was really only designed to fit five to eight drums at the most but we crammed in over thirty. We fitted them all with pumps so we could reach the material in them from the top without tipping them. The entire space was packed, but the drum area was exceptionally bad. We were not thinking big enough when we moved.

Essential Wholesale is currently housed in a 35,000 square-foot, certified organic, and FDA registered facility. However, it is once more out of space and will be moving in 2012 to a 58,000 square-foot space.

The Rest of the Story....

We have had a lot of God moments in our business where we know that only the hand of God could have orchestrated our blessings. One of them was the day we met George Lizer. My parents had come to town to watch our kids so Dennis and I could meet with a potential big client from California. We were certain this was going to be a big break. Only the client never showed up, never called to cancel and avoided our calls. Since I had time without the kids, I decided to take care of an order problem I had experienced at a local supplier that week.

Since we were just blocks away I walked up the street and waited in their will call area to speak with someone. I had ordered amber bottles and lids, but I hadn't been given the right number of lids. An older gentleman was in front of me waiting to speak to them as well. He requested to speak to the owner of the company and explained that he made shampoo, shower gel and conditioner and was interested in giving them a great deal. The customer service rep vanished for a while and came back saying they were not interested.

Because this was one category I hadn't yet mastered, I eagerly gave up my space in line and introduced myself to the gentleman. I told him we owned a tiny cosmetic business down the road and I was interested in his products. He followed me to our place and one of the most important business meetings of our history took place in an impromptu conversation in our 600 square foot facility. George explained that he was a retired millionaire and just loved helping out people in business. He made and sold us his shower gel, shampoo and conditioner five gallons at a time as we could afford them, but he gave us the 200 gallon price giving us the ability to mark up the price. He also provided us with drums of deionized water as well.

14

Not only did George provide us with great products, but he offered us a hand up. It was George's generosity and belief in us that opened the doors for us to move into his building before we ever could have afforded it. We needed the growing room, but we didn't have the income for it. George leased us space for a low minimum payment plus a percentage of our profits, but never took above the going rate for rent. In the end it worked out great for George, but it was his faith in us that gave us assistance that helped us grow. George became our mentor and friend. Recently he confessed he had thought our Essential Wholesale concept would fail, but that he believed in Dennis and I enough that he was willing to risk it and be there to support us into our next venture.

Imagine if I had allowed my fear of change to stifle the dreams that Dennis had for Essential Wholesale and, later, Essential Labs! Now, we have over 4,000 gallons worth of tanks in our tank farm, and when I walk through it and remember all the small batches that I killed myself making, I have to smile. I was afraid of the growth ahead because I envisioned myself making *every ounce of product* when in reality, business growth freed me up and I haven't made an ounce of product outside of the R&D lab for years. Thank God I got myself out of the way of our potential.

Our labs division, created in 2005, and known as Essential Labs, became the private label and contract manufacturing division that specializes in creating custom natural and organic cosmetics, mineral make-up, and personal care items to companies big and small around the world.

The truth is that behind every business success story there is at least one or more business failure story. Dennis and I are no different. As a matter of fact, many investors are hesitant to invest in someone who hasn't failed yet. Our business success story has two major business failures that both preclude and are intertwined with our story.

The Failure of PB&J's Live

The setting was in the kitchen of PB&J's Live on a busy Friday night. It was the winter of 1996. Dennis and I were friends and business partners. Keegan, my son, was four years old and I was a single mother. Dennis was single and a budding serial entrepreneur. The stress level at our restaurant, PB&J's Live, was high. The business was surviving from week to week on the income brought in on Friday and Saturday Comedy nights. I ran the kitchen, and Dennis was in charge of everything else.

Finances were too tight to have a babysitter, so Keegan was tucked in a safe corner within my line of sight. When the orders started coming in that Friday evening, I handed Keegan a box of markers and gave him directions to stay on the milk crate. I could swear that I had also handed him paper to write on, but given what happened next, maybe I forgot? It is likely that I had it in my mind to give him paper and markers, but I had too much on my mind, and the small details must have escaped me. From Keegan's perspective, the only thing missing in the scenario was upon which to color.

Keegan was always content as long as he was near me. He was especially quiet that night and never left the milk crate. At one point, I glanced over and noticed that Keegan was writing on his hand. I thought to myself that I would go stop him once I got the orders started. I was always rushed to get dinner on every table before the comedy act started.

The hours rolled on, and with each glance at Keegan, I noticed a growing marker tattoo expanding on his body. I kept thinking there would be a break in the dinner rush, which would provide the opportunity for me to go stop his body art, but I didn't have a moment to spare as order after order after order piled in. I sent plate after plate out to the dining room. PB&J's Live was hopping, and Keegan was quiet. By the time the final dessert left the kitchen, and I had time to take a hard look at Keegan, I found him, colorful and quiet on the empty milk crate.

Keegan had taken the free opportunity to not only decorate himself from head to toe, but to do so with gusto. He had colored every inch of skin he could reach without taking off his shorts. He had been so detailed in his work that he had colored behind his ears and even inside of them. He was a walking masterpiece. I couldn't be mad because I had watched him do it and hadn't stopped him. I simply had to smile while he explained each detail of his design. It was washable ink, so "no harm, no foul" was my thought.

Sometimes we have to make a judgment call on the things that we give the power to upset us. I could have beaten myself down believing that I had neglected my son. I could have been angry at my circumstances as our business was barely surviving. I could have been mad that I worked all day at a regular job and all night at our business and still didn't have enough money to get a babysitter for my son. But in reality my son was happier with me no matter what I was doing. I had chosen to start a business when I was already financially struggling. I had made choices that resulted in all the events of the night and I chose to not regret the circumstances I found myself in.

However, our business did eventually fail by circumstances outside of our control. Packing our restaurant on Friday and Saturday nights was great for us, but it did not go over well with the other restaurant and a video store with which we shared our parking lot. Our customers took over every space and then some. Not only did we share the same parking lot with these businesses, but we also shared the same landlord. The long-term relationships that the other two businesses had with our landlord outweighed her loyalty to us, and just before Christmas her lawyers sent us a cease-and-desist order. It stated that we could no longer serve hot food, that we couldn't be open at dinner time and that we could no longer provide live entertainment.

The cease-and-desist order was a business killer for us. We had sunk every penny and more into starting up PB&J's Live and had nothing left over to fight for our business or even open our doors for another meal without our menu, dinner service and live entertainment. We had made fatal errors in our contract and our location. We simply had to close our doors, auction off our equipment and walk away with a huge business loss and debt.

Dennis and I may have failed at that business but our friendship led to marriage. We all laugh at the stories of the experiences we had at PB&J's Live now. The markers washed off of Keegan. We all remember how Keegan felt like just as much of an owner of our restaurant as we did - minus the financial stress. He loved to greet people, seat people, and sing on stage before we opened. He was sad to say goodbye to his PB&J's family, and we learned a very expensive business lesson. But in the end, Keegan grew up with Dennis and I as we built, failed, rebuilt, started over, and grew our family businesses.

The Failure of von Natur

When we left Essential Wholesale's 2500 square foot space to move into our current space, we still had a year left on our lease. Dennis had an idea to convert the vacant building into a store, which lead to the idea of a mini spa. Since I was in quite an ambitious phase of my life, I immediately jumped on the band wagon. Between being a wife, mother and business woman, I had felt separated from my creative side, so I saw a mini-spa as an opportunity to give my artistic side a new creative outlet.

The Rest of the Story...
Our mentor and business advisor was on an extended vacation when we made the decision to open up von Natur. When he returned and saw what we had gotten ourselves into he shook his head and told us he would have advised us against it. Mentors, they are important people, but they are most useful when you use them to bounce new ideas off!

Converting an empty warehouse into a store front and mini-spa took an enormous amount of creativity, sweat and labor. In the end, the space was amazing. A local television station even did a feature on the design of the store. The layout was exquisite. The staff was great. The products were selling like gangbusters. Yet, the store was a bottomless money pit that demanded constant time, money and energy. We expanded, redeveloped and redesigned, and around the clock we worked. The spa was eating up our time and Essential Wholesale was suffering from our divided attention.

We tried everything to stop the hemorrhaging. Finally, Dennis called a halt to it all and we shut down the von Natur store and spa. I was devastated because I had invested so much emotional energy into the creative side of the building, the products and into the lives of the people that worked for us. I had to lay everyone off, admit defeat and leave behind the piece of art I had made the building into. Mentally, the spa was eating us alive. Emotionally, I was crushed.

With the spa closed, we put all of our focus into branding a product line. We launched a new look for the product and took it to trade shows. I would describe the look as "one of those things you thought was a good idea at the time." The graphics were splashy, colorful and expensive. In reality, I think the stress we were under made us go a little extreme on our look. Buyers loved our product at trade shows, and they loved the concept of our product line, but they hated our look. Our extreme packaging was a shiny, foil disaster.

On top of that, the product line itself was in chaos. There was no relationship between our packaging and the high quality of the product inside. We had not developed clear product lines, so customers were left guessing which cleanser to use with which toner. We were mid-stream, getting notice from the press and enjoying serving thousands of loyal customers. The products themselves were amazing, but we had packaged them inappropriately. We finally decided to end the product line too. To do this, we had to let go of history and wipe the slate clean.

I could not believe we were starting over again. I dreamed up many creative ways that we could use up the packaging and not lose the money we had invested, but there was no option but to scrap what we had and to start from the beginning. We went back to square one to start fresh and new, licking our wounds and learning from our mistakes. That time around, when we revamped the products, we surrounded ourselves with experts and leaned heavily on their advice and counsel. Our employees helped us redefine the product line from the inside out. They shared our burden and made it bearable.

So why did I run a private label manufacturing company, a bulk manufacturing company and launch a retail store/mini-spa along with a product line, all while trying to be a wife and mom at the same time? Well, I suffered from the "super woman complex." I have been prone to think that I could and should do everything myself. I learned from the experience to delegate, to entrust others with my dreams, my vision and my burdens.

I thought Dennis and I could do it all. Together, we had started Essential Wholesale by ourselves while homeschooling one child, with another child in a back-pack and one in my belly. We worked around the clock for that dream because we had to. Our saving grace is that, when we failed—not once with von Natur, but twice—we were surrounded by a team of people who chose to walk beside us.

We did not open the spa with the intention of learning so many hard lessons. In failure, I was humbled. I learned to let go and embrace the experience and all that it taught me. I learned that failure in business is just that: business failure. It does not equal personal defeat.

We embraced the opportunity to reinvent ourselves, but the opportunity for reinvention only came after financial, physical and emotional breaking. I had created a "whole new me" many times in life. But this time was different. In the case of the spa, I had lost sight of the ultimate goal by only focusing on the playing field that I was on. The spa was the playing field comprised of the employees, the building, and the customers. The goal was to have a successful business. We were not even heading toward the goal, but I was so emotionally wrapped up in the playing field that I fought Dennis when it was time to let go.

I was like a drowning woman flapping frantically for something to stop me from drowning, all the while fighting against the rescue. When I surrendered to the rescue I was so relieved. The burden had been so extreme that even the heavy task of laying people off and closing our doors was a massive relief. Closing the spa was the most logical move we had ever made. Level-headed as I am, I still needed a moment to grieve the failure and the broken relationships and let go. The night before the spa closed I wept privately, but by morning I was all business.

Our lives were changed dramatically in the process of the spa and product lines' multiple false starts, wrong directions and new beginnings. Since we are a married couple in business together, we have had to walk through this process without laying blame on each other. We have had to fail together, change together, start over together and - above all - put our relationship first.

I have been blessed with a husband who has always seen a very big picture. Yes, I was terrified in the beginning of our business because his vision was so huge! I could only see the orders that were in front of me each day. He would talk about our future, and it seemed so unrealistic when it was just the two of us barely making ends meet. I had to let go of my misdirection and follow Dennis' lead toward our mutual vision. We had done that once before when we morphed Essential Wholesale out of our previous business model, and I had the faith in him to follow his lead and stand by his side as we put in the labor and hard work each day.

The spa failure was very painful, though, because it was out in the world for everyone to see. I am extremely private while in pain, but this failure, this forced reinvention, was so very public. At first, I resisted being reinvented because it meant a public admission of failure. It meant that my business which others depended upon for income was going to fold underneath them. I was humiliated by the thought of letting other people down and not meeting their expectations.

The Lessons Learned in Failure

The biggest thing I learned while going through the process of failure is to not fight against it, so my philosophy is to be open to change. Be open to opportunities that come your way. Learn as much as you can from other people's mistakes, and from reading business magazines and books whenever possible. When things aren't working, don't hold onto an idea, a business, or the certain way you did things before.

Sometimes you get side-tracked and lose your focus on the goal. Don't beat yourself up, just allow yourself to refocus and change directions. You have to take a moment to have a pity party, but then let go and get on with the business of starting over.

Equip yourself with the lessons of others, your own life lessons, and a heavy dose of reality. One of the great lessons that I learned from failure was to become vulnerable. There are times in business that you make mistakes. You can't put your failures and mistakes in a bag and carry it around with you, occasionally using them to beat yourself up. The people that I laid off embraced me and faced their new jobless challenge. Many of them are still in my life.

More than anything, don't make any excuses that stop you from changing. For instance, if you want to lose weight you might excuse yourself from your workout one day by saying, "I'm too tired to exercise." However, until you start exercising, you will remain too tired. Once you follow through on your decision to start moving, your energy will be boundless.

My decisions got me to where I am in life. I took ownership of them, and the bitterness that could have grown out of discontent died for lack of nourishment. Don't trip yourself up or hold yourself back with excuses that you invent and hold on to for comfort or for fear of change. Forgive yourself, forgive others, and forgive your circumstances, so that you can be free to move forward and enjoy your journey.

Allow yourself to blossom right where you are and stop waiting for all of your ducks to be in a row. Maybe your ducks won't come together in a straight line at first. I know mine don't. The reality is that tomorrow my ducks could be scattered everywhere, but when I move in one direction, they will follow me. They won't do so in an orderly fashion, and there will be a lot of quacking, but my metaphoric ducks will eventually fall into line behind me as I paddle toward my goals. If I hang back, they hang back; if I throw my hands up in the air and surrender, they scatter. The very best thing for you to do is to move toward your goals and allow your frenzied ducks to follow.

Of course, we all want to move forward and succeed, but what if we could go back? If I found myself back at the beginning, and if I was starting out *then* with what I know *now*, I would live my life exactly the same. However, I wouldn't beat myself up for the chaos I create around me. I wouldn't allow others' disapproval of my creative energy to bother me.

I've never done anything halfway or without passion. If I choose to do something, it is wholeheartedly while I jump in with both feet. I've been known to jump into deep waters with my eyes closed, trusting that not only will I survive, but that I will thrive in the crisis.

I tend to over-commit myself and be stretched thin. I have friends who shake their heads and say, "I don't know how you do it." Well, I don't know how I *wouldn't* do it. If my plate wasn't already full of today's challenges, I would gather up other challenges. It is just my nature.

What is balance to me, is bedlam to another. I've allowed myself to embrace my own sense of balance. At times, there are tipping points that steal my laughter, and I have to fight back to reach my personal equilibrium. As the saying goes, "If mama ain't happy, ain't nobody happy." If I stop laughing and can't find humor even in the chaos, then my life is tipped out of balance, but when I am still laughing, there is still hope in every situation.

As I balance business and family in my own unique way, some might see my life as a state of constant chaos with varying degrees of out-of-control pandemonium. But I have discovered that I blossom right there in the middle of the self-imposed chaos. I operate well inside a world that many wouldn't enjoy. I know that is the case with most entrepreneurs. Rather than reaching for a life vest when we are drowning, we grab onto more of life. When our lives overflow, we are energized and renewed by the experience.

I believe it is healthy to accept who I am and allow myself to be everything God has created me to be even if I'll never fit into a conventional mold. In fact,

I've realized that I can't make my life fit into the world's mold - it doesn't fit. How liberating it was for me to understand that my dreams and aspirations don't have to fit into another person's vision of success! Accepting and loving the person that I am has freed me to experience success beyond my wildest dreams.

When I stopped fighting against myself and my situation, I was free to succeed. For example, our family's focus on business places our children right in the middle, and that is not wrong or right, just different. It is the right path for our family, even if it is different. It is okay to be different.

I have learned to love living out loud, with failure alongside success, experiencing the strain of trials, all while walking beside my husband as we shoulder the burden together of the life we have chosen. I have learned that:

- When my circumstances are not like I imagined they would be … to find peace.
- When my fairy tale image of family is different than I expected… to rejoice in the details of the unexpected.
- When I am in the midst of failure … to get up and start again.
- When life feels like it is spinning out of control … to find my equilibrium and enjoy the adrenaline rush.

I have also learned that my creativity is mobile and not tied to the location in which I create. My creativity is a gift that I can use as a Cosmetic Formulator and Aromatherapist, as an artist and a writer. I don't have to hold on to one piece, one building, or one vision. It is an ever constant source of motivation that can flow into all aspects of my life.

Business and life are both like a canvas. You can wipe it clean and start over again. If you are like me and your strokes are heavy, your canvas will show the evidence of what you have done before. Even a scarred canvas can become something new and beautiful. I am so glad that my canvas can be used and that I can speak from my experienced journey of failure and success to better guide you around the pitfalls and trapdoors in this business.

It is never too late to succeed! Although I am in my forties now, I don't believe I am done growing up. I don't believe I am done succeeding. I still might be that famous poet I've always dreamed of becoming! It is early yet, and I still have a long and adventurous journey ahead of me.

Never be afraid of dreams so big that they cast a giant shadow of fear and doubt.

The Rest of the Story…

When Dennis and I were working night and day and exhausted in every way, we got an offer from a competitor to buy us out. We were a tiny business, barely surviving at the moment, but they wanted to own our formulas. We had several meetings and were given a contract to sign. Dennis and I prayed and thought over the decision.

We were burned out enough to sign it, but we had this glimmer of a dream just outside our reach that made us hesitate. The contract was for fifty thousand dollars along with an employment contract. We were close to signing until Dennis realized if we toughed it out our company would be worth millions one day. We walked into the signing meeting and declined the offer. Our competitor was angry and quickly ushered us out. Needless to say our relationship didn't thrive with that competitor from that day forward, but our business did.

Dennis and I had a dream that was much bigger than us. It included the dreams of our customers and opportunities for our employees. Whenever we wanted to quit we thought how it would impact our employees and our customers. Essential Wholesale became bigger than us and we hired people above our level of abilities to carry us to the next level. In 2011 we sold our company to our management team and a group of investors. It was a win, win, win situation for everyone including our employees and customers.

Chapter 2
Basic Equipment and Packaging

Kitchen Chemistry Equipment

Using the right equipment for your kitchen chemistry projects right from the start will save you time and money. At the company my husband and I founded, Essential Wholesale, they still use many of the same stainless steel pots and utensils we started our business with. Those pots, still useful today, at one time represented entire batches of products and now are only used to warm up a small component in a batch.

Even if you are just interested in making kitchen chemistry projects as a hobby, many of the following equipment tips will still be useful in choosing the right tools you may already have in your kitchen.

Stainless Steel Cooking Pots
A good 2 to 3 gallon (8-14 quarts) stainless steel pot to cook your soap in will be worth every penny you invest. You can find great deals on stainless steel pots and equipment at used restaurant equipment and supply stores. I prefer stainless steel pots over enamel pots. Stainless steel is the easiest material to clean and sanitize prior to use.

Stainless Steel Large Spoons
You will need a good stainless steel spoon for measuring, scraping, stirring and any manual mixing needed to gently release air bubbles.

Accurate Scale
A good scale can save you a lot of heartache in any manufacturing endeavor. Your ingredients should be measured out accurately for every batch. A digital scale is worth the investment. A great scale can measure from 0.002 lbs (0.032 ounce) all the way up to 20 lbs. However, a great scale can be very expensive. Look around for used and reconditioned scales. Another good option is to have two less expensive scales; one that measures all your low weights and a second that can measure higher weights.

Thermometer
You will need a thermometer that can measure up to at least 165 °F or above. My preference is a laser thermometer, but a candy or deep-fry thermometer with a stainless steel tip will work, too.

Immersion Stick Blender
An immersion stick blender, also known as a hand-blender or stick blender, can be found in the kitchen department of any store.

For bigger batches, a wonderful option is to invest in a stainless steel mixer that can be attached to an electronic drill. The motor on the drill will survive longer than an immersion stick blender. An example is a Jiffy Mixer made with rust resistant stainless steel.

Hand Mixer
This will come in handy for the whipped butter recipes included in this book. In general, a hand mixer isn't the right choice for DIY products because it whips air into your products, but with whipped butter that is the goal.

Food Processor
A good food processor comes in handy with powdered products. I find it useful to have a small one as well as a larger one. The small one is perfect for mineral makeup and the bigger one is great for bath products and body powders.

Goggles, Gloves, Mask and Apron
When working with and handling kitchen chemistry projects you should take extra care to protect your hands, eyes and body by wearing gloves. This will protect the product from the germs left on your hands, even after vigorous washing, and protect your hands from direct contact with ingredients at 100% concentrations. You should also wear a mask while mixing dry ingredients that can easily float through the air and into your respiratory system. A hair net should be worn during the manufacturing of all cosmetics to comply with Good Manufacturing Practices (GMP) if you decide to turn your hobby into a business. Even if you are simply making products for personal use and to give as gifts, it is nice to insure your products are contaminant free.

Soap Molds
For making Melt and Pour Soaps and many bath bomb recipes there are a wide variety of soap molds to pick from, including: flexible silicone molds, heavy duty molds, industrial molds and single cavity and trays molds. There are also many items around your house that can be used as soap molds. Any plastic mold will work as long as the sides are flexible and it can withstand warm liquid.

Spray Bottle with Alcohol
During Melt and Pour Soap projects, you will need a spray bottle of denatured alcohol or rubbing alcohol to reduce bubbles. It will also come in handy when you pour the soap in the molds to disperse the small bubbles that occur when pouring.

Spray Bottle with Witch Hazel USP
A spray bottle containing witch hazel USP will come in handy with the majority of the bath bomb and bath fizzy recipes. When making bath bombs a spritz of witch hazel USP creates just enough of a reaction to create a hard outer shell on your bath bombs. Witch hazel USP contains 14% alcohol which allows the witch hazel to evaporate quickly and to insure that the addition of a water phase to your recipe will not cause microbial growth.

Packaging Your Chemistry

In the resource guide at the end of this book I am providing a link to a page on Essential Wholesale's website containing a long list of packaging suppliers. There you will find packaging in every shape and size for hundreds of suppliers. It is important to choose the right packaging and to label correctly.

Packaging Materials
Your packaging options can seem daunting, but with a few tips hopefully I can help you wade through the pluses and minuses of packaging options.

Glass
On the positive side glass makes for classy looking packaging and protects your product from light and air. On the negative side glass can cause your shipping costs to skyrocket, can't be squeezed to remove product, can be dangerous in wet situations like the shower and tend to increase the overall cost of your product.

Aluminum
The upside of aluminum packaging is that it looks great, it protects from light and air, and it is super light-weight. The downside is that it gets damaged easily in shipping. You must count on a good percentage of aluminum packaging to arrive to you damaged, get damaged during filling and get damaged in shipment to your customer.

High-density Polyethylene (HDPE)
The upside of HDPE is that it is inexpensive and light-weight. It is a perfectly fine packaging choice if you are not going to use essential oils. Essential oils have the ability to escape through HDPE packaging. HDPE is commonly used for bottles that house bleach, milk, shampoo, detergent, liners of cereal boxes and grocery bags.

Polyethylene Terephthalate (PET or PETE)
The upside of PET or PETE is that it is light-weight, airtight, is available with UV coating or colored to protect products from light. PET/PETE is the most common recycled plastic.

Packaging of All Shapes and Sizes
Tubes
Packaging in tubes requires a tube filler and sealer. Most home crafters won't have one handy in their home, but in case you private label I wanted to pass on a valuable lesson we learned. If you are going to use tubes you should consider screen printing. Labels crimp, bend and generally start to look messy on a tube with only a few uses.

Malibu Tubes
Malibu tubes are a popular tube option for home crafters. The down side is they are hard to fill and most private label manufacturers won't touch them because they are difficult to automat.

Bottles
Bottles are an excellent option, but you should always consider the viscosity of the product you are putting in them prior to filling them. You can use a disc cap, pump or sprayer on a bottle. If your product is too thick it won't matter what you put on top to get it out.

Jars
Jars are an excellent packaging choice, but again you must always consider the viscosity of the product you are putting in them. If the product is too thin it will slop all over the place and be messy for the consumer. You can chose dome caps, smooth caps or ribbed caps and even ones with seals or no seals.

Airless Packaging
I'm a huge fan of airless packaging. They are great for organically preserved products or anything that is best kept free of air and light. Essential Wholesale has an organically preserved product line that is broad spectrum and stable. However, the products do require special handling and packaging. Air and light can react with these products, so we recommend you package these products in tubes, airless pumps, bottles with pumps or treatment pumps that are opaque or darkly colored.

Foamer Pumps
Foamer pumps combine liquid and air to produce foam without the use of gas propellants. They are a great way to turn liquid castile soap into a viable consumer product. Many consumers do not like how watery thin liquid castile soap is, but with a foamer pump even a dilute castile soap can be appealing to the everyday consumer.

Tips for Filling

The easiest method is to have someone else do it (contract packaging), but that isn't always a viable option. Here a few tips for filling your containers. Remember to ALWAYS thoroughly clean any utensils you use with rubbing or denatured alcohol prior to use.

Pump
One of the easiest methods of filling is to invest in a pump that will fit right onto the bulk packaging you are starting from. You can disassemble the pump and clean it each use, but be sure to sanitize it right before use.

Funnels
Funnels can make your life easy. You can find funnels in the kitchen and automotive department of any store. Don't allow yourself to be limited by the tip of the funnel, feel free to cut the ends to best fit your packaging. You might find that the same funnel can be custom fitted to fit a variety of bottle openings depending on whether or not you cut the tip down. But always remember to spray your funnel down with denatured alcohol before you use it.

Gallon Bags
Gallon ziplock bags can really come in handy for small packaging projects. Simply fill your lotion or crème into the gallon bag, snip a small end off and use it like a frosting bag to fill your jars.

Large Syringe
A large syringe can be used for packaging small quantities of material. I'm not fond of this method because it is just too time consuming to refill the syringe.

What You Say on Your Packaging Matters

Drugs, Aromatherapy and Cosmetics
There is a fine line between drugs, aromatherapy and cosmetics. It is important that as aromatherapy and cosmetic companies we clearly stay on our side of the line and not walk the tightrope between the two definitions. Our job as cosmetic companies is to cleanse and to promote beauty. We have plenty to do inside our own world without tinkering with the drug definitions.

NOTE: All *italics* that follow were added by me as examples and not official FDA comments.

What is a Cosmetic?

A cosmetic is defined in the Federal Food, Drug, Cosmetic Act, Section 201 (i) as being:

"Articles intended to be rubbed (*serums, moisturizers, etc.*), poured (*bubble baths, oils, etc.*), sprinkled (*body powders, bath powders, etc.*), or spray on (*body deodorant, perfumes, body mists, etc.*), introduced or otherwise applied to the human body or any part thereof for cleansing (*cleansers, exfoliants, etc.*), beautifying (*exfoliants, moisturizers, makeup, etc.*), promoting attractiveness (*makeup, perfumes, deodorants, etc.*) or altering the appearance (*cleansers, exfoliants, serums, moisturizers, makeup, etc.*)"

Cosmetics: are not as regulated as drugs. They do not require pre-clearance by FDA, and GMP is not required. Cosmetics have simple labeling regulations, and voluntary adverse effects reporting. You cannot make any claims other than cosmetic usage even if it is accurate or nature's wonder "drug." The Cosmetic Legality Principle does not require pre-market approval or notification of products or ingredients, clearance of products safety, or substantiation of product performance claims (*moisturizing, cleansing, deodorizing, etc.*). Mandatory establishment or product registration is currently voluntary.

Cosmetics exclude soap, but if your soap claims to be "cleansing, beautifying or moisturizing," it is a cosmetic and must be labeled appropriately. This means you are required to include a full International Nomenclature of Cosmetic Ingredients (INCI) ingredient list on every bar of soap and follow all cosmetic regulations ONLY if you make claims that go above and beyond cleansing, beautifying, or moisturizing. The Manufacturer is responsible for making cosmetics safe and they must not be adulterated or misbranded.

Adulterated is defined as harmful or injurious to user under customary conditions of use such as microbiology, unapproved color additive, chemical contaminant or prohibited ingredient.

Misbranded is defined as when labeling is false or misleading; Package does not exhibit labeling information required by statute or regulation; Packaging not in compliance with 1970 Poison Prevention Packaging Act (PPPA). All cosmetic ingredient lists must use INCI (International Nomenclature of Cosmetic Ingredients) names for all cosmetic ingredients in a finished product. The use of trade or common names is not allowed on cosmetic ingredient lists.

What is a Drug?

A Drug is defined in Federal Food, Drug, Cosmetic Act, Section 201 (g) as being:

"Articles intended for use in the diagnosis, cure (*anti-wrinkle, antibacterial, anti-fungal, anti-acne etc.*), mitigation (*pain reliever, headache reducer, muscle relaxant, etc.*), treatment (*acne treatment, fungal treatment, wrinkle cures, psoriasis and eczema, anti-cancer treatments, etc.*) or prevention (*anti-scar, wrinkle cure, cancer prevention, antiperspirant, etc.*), of disease. Articles (*other than food*) intended to affect the structure (*wrinkles, perspiration, scars, etc.*) or any function (*cell regeneration, collagen formation, etc.*) of the body."

Drugs: are highly regulated and require pre-clearance by FDA, and GMP is required. Drugs have highly regulated labeling laws (i.e. Drug Facts). They require reporting of all and any adverse effects known, and they can make proven, specific, and tested claims that follow the monographs requirements. In the Drug Legality Principle, a product meets the definition of drug if it complies with ALL requirements for drugs (even if it also meets the definition of cosmetic). All cosmetics that meet the definition of a drug have to be registered and regulated by the FDA. A product is considered a drug if it makes claims such as being a sunscreen, antibacterial soap, anti-dandruff shampoo, anti-acne, anti-wrinkle, antiperspirant, etc.

"The FDA interprets the term "soap" to apply only when:

- The bulk of the nonvolatile matter in the product consists of an alkali salt of fatty acids and the product's detergent properties are due to the alkali-fatty acid compounds, and
- The product is labeled, sold, and represented solely as soap [21 CFR 701.20]." FDA

What is Soap?

It is very common to find melt and pour soap, as well as true soaps, improperly labeled and containing drug claims. However, most melt and pour soaps do not meet the first standard, because the bulk of the product is not alkali salt and fatty acids.

"If a product intended to cleanse the human body does not meet all the criteria for soap, as listed above, it is either a cosmetic or a drug. For example, if a product consists of detergents or primarily of alkali salts of fatty acids and is intended not only for cleansing but also for other cosmetic uses, such as beautifying or moisturizing, it is regulated as a cosmetic."

Melt and pour soaps consist of detergents and, according to the FDA's definition, they are a cosmetic and not soap. Detergents are essentially de-fatting agents which allows them to remove fats, lipids, dirt, make-up, and debris from the surface of the skin. Detergents aren't bad; they just aren't soap by definition. You are required to include a full International Nomenclature of Cosmetic Ingredients (INCI) ingredient list on every bar of melt and pour soap, and you must follow all cosmetic regulations.

Your Products Intended Use Can Make Your Cosmetic a Drug

Example #1: Product's Intended Use: Drug - A product with any of the following intended uses is a drug: antiperspirant/deodorant (*stops perspirations*), dandruff shampoo (*treats dandruff*), sunscreen/suntan preparation (*prevents sunburn*), fluoride toothpaste (*prevents cavities*), and skin protectants (*helps heal cuts*).

Example #2: Product's Intended Use: Cosmetic - A product with any of the following intended uses is a cosmetic: deodorant (*cover up odor*), shampoo (*cleanse hair*), suntan preparations (*moisturized while tanning*), toothpastes (*cleans teeth or freshens breath*), skin protectants (*moisturize skin*).

Notice that both the ingredients and the intended use of the product make a difference in whether it is considered a drug or a cosmetic.

Three Types of Claims that Can Cause Your Cosmetic to be a Drug
1. *Claims that suggest physiological change*—For instance, if you say "younger looking" rather than "younger" you are a cosmetic. If you say "removes" or "prevents" wrinkles, rather than "covers" your product is a drug.
2. *Claims that sound scientific*—For instance, if you claim your soaps are "Compounded in our laboratory under the most sterile conditions," or "If blemishes persist, see a doctor," your products is a drug.
3. *Claims that appear in an applicable OTC monograph*—Sunscreen products, hormone products, acne, eczema, psoriasis, skin bleaching, etc. Even implied claims by known effects of ingredients. For example, with skin bleaching products, the presence of many ingredients automatically make your product a drug. Remember that even if a cosmetic has a drug action, it must qualify as a drug first and then a cosmetic.

If an ingredient has a monograph it automatically makes a product a drug with the intended use as described in the monograph. The FDA has published monographs for OTC ingredients stating what ingredients can be used and their intended use. Using those ingredients in a product makes your cosmetic a drug—no ifs, ands or buts about it. Remember, if you use an ingredient with a monograph, that product then meets the definition of a drug, and it must comply with ALL requirements for drugs (even if it also meets the definition of cosmetic).

Are You Transforming Your Cosmetic Into a Drug?

The trick is this, it doesn't matter whether the claim is true or not, it's whether the claim transforms the cosmetic into a drug. You might know your aromatherapy helps lighten hyper-pigmentation, your ointment helps cure eczema and your serum irons out wrinkles, but as soon as you state or imply that fact on your label, in your literature, in any print advertisement, on your website, or anywhere else, you are placing your product into the drug category. Therefore, you must follow all drug regulations and present your product to the FDA before it hits the market. You will also need to present case studies to the FDA to back up your claim. For more information on this, go to The Center for Drug Evaluation and Research (CDER) homepage.

Labeling Tips

On the Label

All cosmetic labels are required by law to have the following:

- You must identify the manufacturer or distributor (by name) of the product and have a way for the customer to reach them. Use company name, address and phone number.

- You must list the ingredients in the order they appear in your formula. The ingredients must be identified by their botanical (INCI) name. A marketing description and use of the product is nice, as is the fragrance name, but it is not required unless the product use is not obvious or you are exporting to another country.

- The Department of Weights and Measures requires the actual weight of the product both in standard and metric to be disclosed on the label. Metric should be first to comply with European Union (EU) requirements.

- Include any warning statements needed or required by law as with bubble baths or products containing Alpha Hydroxy Acids. IE: "Warning: Not for use in or around eyes."

About the Label

- It is imperative for your label company to make sure the right adhesive is used for your packaging.

- It is always a good idea to UV-coat or varnish your labels if they will be shipped or handled with wet hands. Also, paper labels should be coated with a UV or similar coating to avoid "scuffing" of the label in transport. It is preferable for toiletries with paper labels to have a coating to guard against smearing when in contact with moisture. An uncoated label will almost certainly be damaged by an essential oil.

- Clear labels have a great shelf appeal and look professional, but they do have a few pitfalls, i.e. any surface flaw in the bottle will show, dust, oils and fingerprints are all likely to cause poor adhesion.

- UPC Codes: Your label company can help you establish your UPC numbers. These are not required by law, but some larger retailers prefer that you have them. For more information and details check out their website at www.uc-council.org.

- If you use a private label company make sure they see and approve the shape and size of your labels prior to price quoting and scheduling a production run. Odd shapes or larger sizes may not fit on most machines and may require hand labeling, which is more expensive, but possible. It is best to know all these factors up front.

Storage Tips

All products should be stored in a cool, dark place with a stable and consistent temperature. Typical room temperature is 68-77 °F (20-25 °C), which is the perfect storage temperature for cosmetics. When cosmetics of any kind are stored at higher temperatures the preservative system is significantly deteriorated. One day of a cosmetic stored in a warm area is equal to about four days of the product shelf life.

Chapter 3
Ingredients

The Language and Roadmap

All cosmetic ingredient lists must use INCI (International Nomenclature of Cosmetic Ingredients) names for all cosmetic ingredients in a finished product. The use of trade or common names is not allowed on cosmetic ingredient lists. INCI names are uniform scientific names and are mandated on the ingredient statement of every consumer personal care product. In this chapter I will give you both the common name and the INCI name.

INCI is an international designation for the declaration of the ingredients on the packaging of cosmetics. The use of INCI minimizes the language barriers that often hinder consumer understanding and international trade. The INCI names are allocated by the American Cosmetic Association, Personal Care Products Council and are used internationally. The adoption of INCI terminology ensures cosmetic ingredients are consistently listed using the same ingredient name from product to product.

In the U.S., the FDA requires all cosmetics include a listing of ingredients using the standardized INCI name for each ingredient in descending order. INCI ingredient names on product labels allow consumers to easily compare the ingredients between multiple products, using a common language. INCI ensures transparency in cosmetic ingredient disclosure.

INCI is required in America under the Food, Drug, and Cosmetic Act and the Fair Packaging and Labeling Act. In Canada INCI is required by Food and Drugs Act and Cosmetic Regulations. The declaration of the ingredients in accordance with the INCI system has been a legal requirement in the European Union since 1993. The declaration of ingredients in cosmetics with the INCI name is always required to be in descending order.

There are some that claim that "if you can't pronounce it, it can't be good for you" in reference to cosmetic ingredients. This statement from a banner at Natural Products Expo was made by the Environmental Working Group should take the award as the most uninformed, illogical statement ever made by a political action group. It simply proves they have no business attempting to be experts in the field of cosmetics and personal care that they attempt to be with their fatally flawed Skin Deep Database. If only they knew the simple fact that the cause for difficult to pronounce words in cosmetic labeling is due to internationally standardization to ensure consumer safety worldwide. I still can't say *Butyrospermum parkii*, but Shea Butter is as safe as ingredients come.

Whether you can pronounce the INCI term or not, the use of INCI nomenclature is the law. Always, always, always include any ingredients that you add to your recipes on the ingredient list. This means if you add lemon essential oil to scent a body spray, Yellow 5 to color a bath bomb or poppy seeds as an exfoliant to Melt and Pour Soap, all of the added ingredients must be included on the product ingredient list.

Salts

Atlantic Fine Sea Salts
INCI: Sodium Chloride
Sea salts soften the water and can be used for a cleansing, abrasive exfoliate and help draw toxins from the body. People worldwide have used the healing power of salts baths for centuries. The minerals and trace elements deep clean and revitalize the body. Atlantic sea salt is produced using the ancient method of solar evaporation in a region that is free of pollution and has high evaporation rates.

Dead Sea Salts
INCI: Sodium Chloride
Dead Sea salt is salt dried from the Dead Sea. Dead Sea salts are available in fine and course grades, which give you a nice variety of visual choices for your bath salts. Dead Sea salts have a high mineral content is used for treating and preventing various diseases such as psoriasis, acne, and rheumatism. Dead Sea salt is beneficial to the skin and the rest of the body, because the skin absorbs salt, vitamins, and other substances into the body.

People come from far and wide to bathe in hot springs, mineral baths, and the Dead Sea because of the unique mineral compositions of each place. In Israel, the Dead Sea attracts visitors because it is the lowest point on the earth and contains a high percentage of natural minerals. In many countries people with conditions labeled "incurable" have reduced their symptoms or completely resolved them after being treated with mineral hydrotherapy

Dendritic Salt
INCI: Sodium Chloride
Dendritic salt is a fine-grain salt which has been crystallized to provide more surface area and irregular surfaces. This is desirable in bath salts because the increased surface area helps retain fragrance, requires fewer pigments and reduces clumping. This natural salt absorbs essential oils twice as efficiently as other salts used in bath mixes. It's specially formulated to prevent caking, add

flow-ability and to keep the scent in your salts longer. I recommend using one cup of dendritic salt to every 20 cups of other salts used.

Epsom Salt
INCI: Magnesium sulfate
Epsom salt is a chemical compound containing magnesium, sulfur, and oxygen. Medical research indicates that magnesium may reduce inflammation and relieve pain, making it beneficial in the treatment of sore muscles, migraine headaches and fibromyalgia. Soaking in an Epsom Salt bath is one of the most effective means of making the magnesium that your body needs readily available. The best method for making an Epsom Salt soak is to add two cups of Epsom Salt to warm water in the bathtub and soak for 12 to 15 minutes. For a foot bath, add one cup of Epsom Salt to a tub of warm water and soak.

According to the Epsom Salt Council, the magnesium in Epsom salt helps ease stress, improves sleep and concentration, helps muscles and nerves function properly, reduces inflammation to relieve pain and muscle cramps, and improves oxygen use. And the sulfates in Epsom salts help flush toxins, improve absorption of nutrients, and help prevent or ease migraine headaches.

Himalayan Salts
INCI: Sodium Chloride
Himalayan salts contain 84 beneficial trace elements and have a unique crystal structure. Pink Himalayan Salt is mined from ancient sea beds inside the Himalayan Mountains. Himalayan salts are completely unrefined, raw, and remain in their natural form. Himalayan salts are pure and free of contaminants and pollutants. The pink color of the salts comes from the high content of Iron. Himalayan salts are said to contain trace amounts of 84 minerals and elements including potassium, magnesium, calcium, iodine, zinc, and sodium.

These coarse-grain salts make excellent additions to bath salt blends and are used at 100% of the salt portion of a formula. For thousands of years, the salt has been used as a main ingredient in baths, body scrubs, drinks, and foods and has been revered for its unique crystalline beauty and its folk-medicinal properties.

Solar Salt
INCI: Sodium Chloride
Solar salt is an extra-coarse white crystalline form of sodium chloride that is produced by the solar evaporation of seawater from the Great Salt Lake. The salt crystals are refined by washing with clean saturated brine to remove surface impurities, then drained of excess moisture, dried and screened to size.

The appearance of solar salts is a good enough reason to add them to your recipes to give texture to your product, but they also contain minerals that are unique to the extremely saline Great Salt Lake.

Sugars

Refined Sugar
INCI: Sucrose
Sugar is refined from sugar cane and sugar beet through the repeated process of washing, boiling, centrifuging, filtering and drying.

Turbinado Sugar
INCI: Sucrose
Turbinado Sugar, also known as sugar in the raw, is natural cane turbinado sugar that is grown and cut in the tropics and less processed than refined sugar.

Clays

Bentonite Clay
INCI: Bentonite
Bentonite clay is a combination of montmorillonite and volcanic ash. Montmorillonite is a soft phyllosilicate group of minerals found in the Midwestern United States and in Canada. It is highly absorbent clay that pulls oils and toxins from the skin. Bentonite Clay is the best clay to use in a soak, because it increases the rate of detoxification. To ensure that your customers don't detoxify too quickly, I recommend using only one pound or less of bentonite in a 20 to 30 minute soak. There are many who recommend higher concentrations of bentonite clay to bath water, but with the addition of aromatherapy this is not necessary. To create a relaxing and detoxifying treatment with Bentonite clay soak, add lavender, juniper, cedarwood (*Cedrus deodora*) or cypress essential oils. For example: To 1 lb. bentonite clay add 30 drops lavender + 30 drops cedarwood (*Cedrus deodora*) + 10 drops cypress + 10 drops juniper essential oils and mix.

Bentonite clay is a wonderful example of how injecting lab animals with safe cosmetic ingredients can produce bad scientific data. Bentonite clay is commonly used in cosmetics and some people even consume it, but when it is injected into rats it is fatal for the rat. That data, in the hands of an organization with an agenda, could be used to incorrectly label bentonite clay as "dangerous." Misrepresentation of the safety of cosmetic ingredients has been done many times on perfectly safe cosmetic ingredients in order to promote an organization's cause.

Green Clay
INCI: Montmorillonite
Green clay is from a subcategory of clay minerals known as illite clay, which often occur intermixed with kaolinite clays. The green color of the clay comes from a combination of iron oxides and decomposed plant matter, mostly kelp seaweed and other algae. The mineral montmorillonite is a component of green clay, as well as other minerals including: dolomite, magnesium, calcium, potassium, manganese, phosphorus, zinc, aluminum, silicon, copper, selenium, and cobalt.

Green clay is regarded as a useful treatment for stimulating the skin and removing impurities from the epidermis. Clay soaks are great because they adsorb impurities from the skin cells, causing dead cells to slough off. Clay tones by stimulating the flow of blood to the epidermis. Green clay produces a slight cooling effect on the skin, constricts follicles, and deep cleanses the epidermis. It is very absorbent and cleansing to the skin sebum.

Green clay is rich in calcium, magnesium, potassium, and sodium. It energizes the connective tissue. It is antiseptic and healing. It gently stimulates and is effective in increasing the lymph flow and circulation, enabling oxygen, and speeding the elimination of wastes. Green clay has a high mineral content. Green Clay can be added to a bath soak from 0.5 to 50% of the recipe.

Kaolin Clay
INCI: Kaolin
Kaolin clay originally came from the Kaoling Hill in Kiangsi Providence in China. It is a white powder, insoluble in water and absorbent. It absorbs oils secreted from the skin and draws out impurities and toxins through absorption. It is great to add to a soak after insect bites and stings. It is composed of silica, iron, magnesium, calcium, sodium, zinc and other minerals. Kaolin clay has an electromagnetic quality and attracts oils and particles left on the skin. Kaolin clay can be added to a bath soak from 0.5 to 100% of the recipe.

Pink Clay
INCI: Kaolinite
Pink clay is rich in trace elements and used to detoxify and cleanse the face and body. It is composed of silica, iron, magnesium, calcium, sodium, zinc and other minerals. Because pink clay can easily stain linens I recommend using just a hint of pink clay in your recipes.

Rhassoul Clay
INCI: Moroccan Lava Clay
Rhassoul clay's most impressive properties in skin improvement are its

capacity of absorption due to its high level of ion exchange. In addition to its oil removal characteristics, rhassoul clay masks certainly have the ability to smooth and improve dry skin. Rhassoul clay has been used for over 12 centuries by populations from North Africa, South Europe and the Middle East.

Clinical studies have been conducted by two different research laboratories in the United States to evaluate rhassoul clay masks on skin conditions. The study results showed that a single use of our rhassoul clay mask reduces dryness and flakiness; and improves skin clarity, elasticity and/or firmness and skin texture.

Powders

Allantoin
INCI: *Allantoin*
Allantoin is present naturally in comfrey plant and the urine of most mammals. It is a nature-identical, safe, non-toxic chemical compound that is used for its healing, soothing, and anti-irritating properties. It has the ability to help heal wounds and sores, and it stimulates the growth of healthy tissue. Allantoin is a skin softener and an anti-irritant, which inhibits allergic type responses. In bath soaks it is traditionally used at 1% or less of a recipe.

Aloe Powder
INCI: *Aloe vera barbadensis miller*
Aloe powder is freeze-dried, cryo-dried, or spray-dried aloe powder with deionized water to a single strength equivalency (SSE). Once the aloe powder is reconstituted, the finished product requires preservatives in order to remain stable, which is why using aloe powder in a bath soak is so wonderful. It requires no preservation because the bath soak has a single-use application.

There are many different aloe powders available on the market today. I prefer 100 % pure aloe vera that is International Aloe Science Council certified. The IASC is a third-party verification process that ensures purity of aloe products. The aloe that we use comes from freshly harvested leaves of the *Aloe vera barbadensis miller* variety of aloe. The inner gel (a.k.a. fillet) is carefully removed to minimize disruption of the aloin layer. The resulting gel is processed to remove the pulp and fiber. The gel is then pasteurized to maintain efficacy and concentrated using low temperature evaporation. The gel concentrate is then freeze-dried without the use of matrix, preservatives or any other additives. The finished concentrate allows us to follow an exact formula to reconstitute the aloe to a single strength equivalency (SSE) aloe juice. Because aloe powder is so concentrated, it can be easily used at less than 0.5% in any bath soak recipe.

Blue Green Algae
INCI: *Aphanizomenon flos aquae*
Blue green algae powder comes from the Klamath Falls in Oregon. It is the purest, most nutrient intact algae available in the world. It is a wild-harvested, organic-certified, single-celled organism which occurs in the remote area of the Oregon Cascade Mountains. It is highly bio-available and contains a full spectrum of minerals: chlorophyll, B vitamins, beta-carotene, pro vitamin A, lipids, active enzymes, essential amino acids, nucleic acids, DHA, and EPA fatty acids. Because blue green algae powder is so concentrated and dark in color, it can be easily used at less than 0.5% in any bath soak recipe.

Borax
INCI: Sodium Borate
Borax a.k.a sodium borate is a boron compound, mineral and salt of boric acid. It is commonly used in detergents, household cleaning supplies, as a buffering agent in biochemical and chemical laboratories, a food additive in some countries (banned in the US), cosmetic emulsifier used by crafters (on Canada's Prohibited and Restricted Cosmetic Ingredient list), fire retardant, insecticide, used in fertilizers and other industrial purposes. In this book Borax is only used in household cleaning recipes. I do not subscribe to the common belief it can and/or should be used as an emulsifier.

Borax comes from both natural sources and lab created sources. It occurs over time naturally in evaporate deposits produced by evaporation of seasonal lakes. It is also synthetically produced from other boron compounds. Borax converts some water (H_2O) molecules to hydrogen peroxide (H_2O_2) making it a highly effective cleaning agent. It is used as a buffering agent because it has a pH of about 9.5. Borax is a stable product, but when heated it loses water, eventually forming anhydrous borax. Incompatible materials and conditions to avoid include reaction with strong reducing agents, such as metal hydrides or alkali metals, which will generate hydrogen gas, which could create an explosive hazard.

The Prohibited and Restricted Cosmetic Ingredient List in Canada says, "Permitted at concentrations equal to or less than 5%. The inner and outer label of the cosmetic shall carry cautionary statements to the effect: "Do not use on broken or abraded skin", "Not to be used by children under three years of age." Warnings are not required where sodium borate is used as a pH adjuster, and the concentration is equal to or less than 0.1%."

The CIR Expert Panel, "The safety of Sodium Borate and Boric Acid has been assessed by the Cosmetic Ingredient Review (CIR) Expert Panel. The CIR Expert Panel evaluated the scientific data and concluded that Sodium Borate and Boric Acid, in concentrations less than or equal to 5%, are safe as cosmetic ingredients. The CIR Expert Panel also cautioned that cosmetics and personal care products containing free Sodium Borate or Boric Acid at 5% should not be used on infant skin or injured skin. In 2003, as part of the scheduled re-evaluation of ingredients, the CIR Expert Panel considered available new data on Sodium Borate and Boric Acid and reaffirmed the above conclusion."

Calcium Sulfate
INCI: Calcium Sulfate
Calcium is a white salt $CaSO_4$ that occurs especially as anhydrite, gypsum, and plaster of Paris and that in hydrated form is used as a building material and in anhydrous form is used as a drying agent.

Corn Starch
INCI: *Zea mays*
Cornstarch is a silky powdery starch made from corn. Use it in body powders, milk baths, and bath bombs to add silkiness and to soothe the skin. Cornstarch is a safer alternative than using talc on babies. It can be added to diaper area barrier creams to keep the skin dry and protected from moisture.

Crème of Tartar is the common name for potassium hydrogen tartrate, which is an acid salt commonly used in cooking. In bubble bars and foaming bath bombs it is used to stabilize the foaming action during use of the product.

Goat Milk
INCI: Goat's Milk Powder
Goat milk leaves the skin with a hydrated appearance, feeling silky smooth. Upon absorption, the milk smoothes, firms and softens the skin. Milk has a long standing in beauty history. Goat milk, in particular, is a natural emollient, containing vitamins A, B6, B12 and E. It contains three times more beta-casein than cow's milk. Goat milk can be added to a bath soak from 0.5 to 50% of the recipe.

Lactose
INCI: Lactose
Lactose is present in the milk of mammals. Lactose leaves the skin feeling silky smooth, with a hydrated appearance. Upon being easily absorbed, the disaccharide smoothens, firms and softens the skin. Milk has a long standing in beauty history.

MSM
INCI: Methylsulfonylmethane
Methylsulfonylmethane is a naturally occurring nutrient found in plants, meats, dairy products, fruits, and vegetables. MSM is therefore found in the normal human diet. It is an odorless, tasteless, white water-soluble, crystalline

solid in its purified form. Your bath soak recipes can incorporate up to 5% MSM in it.

MSM supplies sulfur to the body which allows it to heal itself. It produces muscle relaxation and reportedly a whole host of beneficial qualities. It has been used with great success in eliminating chronic back pain, muscle pain, and repairing cut, scraped, burned, and damaged skin. We've seen reports of MSM eliminating wrinkles, brown spots, skin tumors, and spider veins. MSM is being used for burn victims and for repairing scar tissue. Many people report relief from allergies after using MSM. Other reports indicate that MSM will remove parasites from the body and help the body to detoxify itself.

MSM is anti-inflammatory and antimicrobial. MSM feeds the formation of collagen and elastin while preventing and reducing cross-linking between cells, which is the primary cause of wrinkles and scar tissue. MSM is a natural sulfur compound that contributes to healthy skin, hair and nails. MSM has been used orally and topically to aid skin disorders. When used topically, in the form of a cream or lotion, sulfur is helpful in treating skin disorders including acne, psoriasis, eczema, dermatitis, dandruff, scabies, diaper rash and certain fungal infections.

Mustard Powder
INCI: *Sinapis alba*
Mustard has been used for many years by cultures around the world due to its reputation to increase circulation and open pores. It is thought to stimulate sweating, which, in turn, helps the body rid itself of toxins. Mustard soaks are a staple for me during cold and flu season. Because of the aroma of the mustard I recommend limiting amount to 1% mustard powder in your soaks.

Sea Kelp
INCI: *Ascophyllum nodosum*
Sea Kelp grows deep in the cold sub-tidal waters and it is responsibly harvested, dried and milled following organic standards. It is a yellowish-green colored powder with a fish-like, seaweed odor and flavor. The medicinal part is the stem-like part of the thallus, which is reminiscent of root, leaf or stem-like organs. It grows in the North Atlantic Sea. Sea kelp contains Chlorophyll which helps detoxify the skin and body, essential fatty acids which improve skin elasticity, and carbohydrates which stimulate the skin's ability to heal, and Vitamin A that normalize skin cells. Sea kelp contains proteins and amino acids which are the building blocks of cells and act as skin conditioners. Because of the strong odor of sea kelp I recommend using less than 1% in a bath soak recipe.

Sodium Bicarbonate

INCI: Sodium Bicarbonate

Common Name: Baking Soda

Sodium bicarbonate is better known as baking soda and is used in all kinds of bath soaks, bath bombs, and fizzies. It is a natural alkaline that neutralizes acids and washes away oils and dirt. Its natural pH balance leaves the skin soft, silky and smooth. Sodium bicarbonate often makes up the bulk of a bath soak and up to 95% of a recipe.

Titanium Dioxide

INCI: Titanium dioxide

Titanium Dioxide is a naturally occurring mineral derived from oxide of titanium. It is used to impart whiteness to color cosmetics and personal care products that are applied to the skin, to increase the opacity, and reduce the transparency of a finished product. Titanium Dioxide is used in White Melt and Pour Soap to create the white color. You will also find it in other Melt and Pour Soaps on the market to impart a white color, such as Shea Butter and Goat's Milk bases.

Titanium Dioxide is an important ingredient used in sunscreen products. Sunscreens are regulated by the FDA as Over-The-Counter (OTC) drug products. But this doesn't mean you should say your soap acts as a sunscreen! First of all, it doesn't since it is a wash off product. And secondly, making a sunscreen claim would put your soap under OTC drug regulations.

The FDA has assessed the safety of Titanium Dioxide as a color additive for use in food, drugs and cosmetics. The FDA set regulations approving the Titanium Dioxide for each of these purposes. As a cosmetic, the FDA has stated, "The color additive titanium dioxide may be safely used in cosmetics, including cosmetics intended for use in the area of the eye, in amounts consistent with good manufacturing practice."

According to the Cosmetics Directive of the European Union, Titanium Dioxide is listed as Colour Index (CI) No. 77891 in the Cosmetics Directive of the European Union as an allowed color additive (Annex IV, Part I), and may be used without restriction according to the purity requirements that have been established for the quality of the same material used in foods. Europe also allows Titanium Dioxide to be used as a sunscreen active ingredient to protect against the adverse effects of ultraviolet radiation found in sunlight.

Zinc Oxide

INCI: Zinc Oxide

Zinc oxide is used medicinally as an astringent, antiseptic, skin protective, and to encourage healing. It works wonderfully as an antiperspirant. Zinc Oxide is a physical UV filter. Zinc oxide is a protective substance which can be used as a sun block. Zinc oxide provides near complete opacification to the sun's rays. Several products containing this have wonderful protective properties against the sun, and should be used by people who are extraordinarily sun sensitive.

Butters

Almond Butter
INCI: *Prunus amygdalus dulcis (and) Hydrogenated Vegetable Oil*
Almond butter is derived from sweet almonds specifically from the Mediterranean area, and it is obtained by cold pressing selected fruits followed by a full refining process. The natural oil contains essential fatty acids, but also contains unsaponifiables as natural waxes or paraffin, which are collected during the refining and deodorization process. In cosmetic preparations, the feel and behavior of almond butter is somewhat similar to that of shea butter (*Butyrospermum parkii*). Almond butter exhibits excellent spread-ability on the skin, making it ideal as a massage butter or carrier for treatment products. It adds moisturizing attributes to creams, lotions and bar soaps.

Avocado Butter
INCI: *Persea gratissima (and) Hydrogenated Vegetable Oil*
Avocado butter has been found to significantly increase the water-soluble collagen content in the dermis skin layer. This rich and nourishing butter deeply penetrates into deep skin tissue. It is rich in vitamins A, B1, B2, and D, lecithin, and potassium as well as Vitamin E. This is one of the natural butters that is most easily absorbed by the skin and transported deep into the tissue. It's wonderful emollient properties make it ideal for dry, dehydrated, or mature skins. Furthermore, it also helps to relieve the dryness and itching of psoriasis and eczema. It is also high in sterolins, which help to reduce age spots and help heal sun damage and scars.

Avocado butter is obtained from the fruit of the avocado tree which grows in sub-tropical regions of the world. The butter is created from the avocado fruit oil through a unique hydrogenation process, which yields a soft, greenish butter. It has a mild odor and excellent melting properties which make it suitable for skin care.

Capsicum Butter
INCI: *Cocos nucifera* (Organic Coconut) Oil, *Elaesis guineesis* (Palm) Kernel Oil, Capsicum.
Capsicum butter offers a hot, soothing sensation when used on the skin. This butter, when used correctly in a formulation, can supply a great feeling of relaxation on tired or sore muscles.

Cocoa Butter

INCI: *Theobroma cacao*

Cocoa Butter is a very rich butter, with excellent emollient properties and is used with great effect on very dry, dehydrated, and flaky skin. It easily absorbs into the skin and imparts sheen. Cocoa butter is the solid fat expressed from the roasted seed of the cocoa seed (beans). The cocoa tree is cultivated in most tropical countries and is native to South America. It is highly protective and acts as water repellant. Cocoa butter contains about 5 IU of vitamin E per ounce. Cocoa Butter softens and lubricates the skin. It has the aroma of chocolate. Some people find the scent overwhelming in recipes and prefer to use deodorized cocoa butter.

Hemp Seed Butter

INCI: *Cannabis Sativa Seed Oil and Hydrogenated Vegetable Oil*

Hemp seed butter is produced using the fatty fractions and unsaponifiables (natural waxes/paraffin's) which are collected during the refining processes which are blended with hydrogenated vegetable oil to produce a butter-like material suitable for use in cosmetics and toiletries. Hemp seed butter is made from expeller-pressed non-sterilized and non-fumigated seeds of the hemp plant.

Hemp seed oil has a high content of essential fatty acids, which help the action of hydro lipid coat, thereby reducing trans-epidermal water loss. Hemp seed oil possesses one of the highest PUFA contents of all the natural oils. It provides the four essential fatty acids beneficial to the skin: LA, GLA, LNA, and SDA—one of the highest EFA contents.

Hemp seed butter is often used in body care, soaps, facial creams, lotions, and sunscreens to impart moisture, particularly for dry, damaged skin. Hemp seed oil is one of the "driest" natural oils which are absorbed quickly into the skin, and hence the butter produced from it also exhibits a relatively dry feel. It provides excellent lubrication without being greasy.

Illipe Butter

INCI: *Shorea stenoptera*

Illipe butter is a harder butter with a higher melting point than most other exotic butters, yet it still melts on contact with the skin. The first inhabitants of Borneo (the Dayaks) have been making "butter" from illipe nuts for many centuries for therapeutic and cosmetic purposes. Illipe butter has long-lasting moisturizing attributes. It is most renowned for its skin-softening quality.

The illipe tree grows in the forests of Borneo. The tree grows from 5 to 15 meters in height, with 5 centimeter seeds. The seeds are enclosed in a thin shell with wing-like attachments that enable the seed to fall away from the mother tree. The seeds are collected from the ground and dried in the sun until the shells are sufficiently brittle to be separated from the seeds by pounding in rice mortars.

Illipe's chemical composition closely resembles that of cocoa butter, yet with a slightly higher melting point, making it ideal for use in bar soaps, lip balms, lip sticks, and other stick-type applications where a higher melting point is desired.

Kokum Butter
INCI: *Garcinia Indica*
This butter is obtained from the Indian tree *Garcinia indica*. It is used in skin care products because of its ability to soften skin and is effective on ulcerations and fissures of lips, hands and soles of feet. It helps reduce degeneration of the skin cells and restores elasticity.

Mango Butter
INCI: *Mangifera Indica*
Mango butter is obtained from the kernels of the mango tree. It has a high content of stearic acid which makes it similar to cocoa butter in properties, but this butter is soft not hard. It has only been refined once thus leaving it in more pure state as opposed to the harder Mango Butters sold by competitors. It has good emolliency and lends a protective effect against the sun. It is said to prevent drying of the skin and formation of wrinkles. It reduces degeneration of skin cells and restores flexibility.

Carrier Oils

Almond Oil, Sweet
INCI: *Prunus amygdalus dulcis*
Sweet Almond Oil is pressed from almond kernels. The almond tree is cultivated in Southern Europe, the Mediterranean countries and California. It consists mainly of oleic acid (69%), essential unsaturated fatty acids (25%), sterolins (0.5 to 1%) and vitamin E (about 10 IU per ounce.) It is a light and nearly odorless oil. Sweet almond oil is said to have great nutritional value for all skin types. It has a similar make up to baby sebum, the oil naturally produced by the skin to protect a newborn's skin, and it is easily absorbed. It contains glucosides, minerals, and vitamins and is rich in protein. Sweet almond oil has very little natural smell and can be used as a perfume base. It was highly valued by the Egyptians for cosmetic purposes.

Avocado Oil

INCI: *Persea Americana*

Avocado oil is excellent for dry and wrinkled skin as it moisturizes, nourishes, and softens. It has been found to significantly increase the water-soluble collagen content in the dermis skin layer. Avocado oil contains protein, vitamins A, D, and E, and some amino acids.

Avocado oil is made from the pulp of the avocado fruit. It is a rich, heavy but penetrating oil that is full of nutritive and therapeutic components. Avocado oil contains more than 20% essential unsaturated fatty acids. It contains vitamins A, C, D, and E, proteins, beta-carotene, lecithin, fatty acids, and the "youth mineral" potassium. Avocado oil is high in unsaponifiables (sterolins) which are reputed to be beneficial in reducing age spots, healing scars and moisturizing the upper layers of the skin. Unsaponifiables are a large group of compounds called plant steroids or sterolins. They soften the skin, have superior moisturizing effects on the upper layer of the skin, and reduce scars. The sterolins in avocado oil have been found to diminish age spots. Oils with the highest unsaponifiables are shea butter, avocado oil, sesame oil, soybean oil, and olive oil.

A 1991 study at the Department of Food Engineering and Biotechnology, Technion-Israel Institute of Technology found that treatment with avocado oil significantly increases the water-soluble collagen content in the dermis, which effects the age of the skin. Avocado is used in many folk medicines as an aphrodisiac. Avocado oil is an emollient and very stable. According to the American Medical Association (AMA) Committee on Coetaneous Health it does help make the skin feel softer and smoother, while reducing roughness, cracking, and irritation. Avocado oil may retard the fine wrinkles of aging and is said to help protect the skin from ultraviolet rays.

Borage Oil

INCI: *Borago officinalis*

Borage oil is produced from a wildflower commonly known as the starflower. The plant is large with blue star-shaped flowers. It grows wild all over the world, but mostly throughout Europe and North Africa. Borage has been naturalized to North America as well. It is grown and harvested for herbal use, but mostly for the oil found in the seeds.

Borage oil is a rich source of the essential fatty acid gamma linolenic acid (GLA). The GLA of borage oil is 24% which makes it the richest known source in the world. Borage oil contains polyunsaturated essential fatty acids which aid in the flexibility of the cell membranes and helps normalize trans-epidermal water loss.

In skin care, borage oil is useful because it has a cooling, calming, and diuretic effect on the skin. It soothes damaged, irritated and inflamed skin which makes it a prime candidate for blemished, mature, sun-damaged and troubled skin. Borage oil is emollient and promotes healthy skin. It contains tannins which gives borage oil a minor tightening effect on the skin while restoring moisture without leaving an oily barrier on the skin.

Borage oil capsules is highly recommended for consumption due to the fact that consuming linoleic acid (LA) gives the body the starting material to produce on its own gamma linolenic acid (GLA). Biochemically LA is converted into GLA by the enzyme Delta-6-Desaturase and further transformed into prostaglandin 1 which is beneficial to maintaining healthy skin and suppresses inflammation of the skin. Inflammation of the skin equals diseased skin and only healthy skin can look radiant.

Broccoli Oil
INCI: *Brassica oleracea Italica*
Broccoli seed oil is a perfect ingredient in formulas in which you need exceptional lubricity with a non-greasy feel. The oil is a good emollient in cosmetic products including lip balms, skin creams, and hair care products. Broccoli seed oil can effectively be used as an all-natural alternative to silicone in shampoos and conditioners. It has a unique feel as well as a penetrating ability to impart a natural, healthy shine to skin and hair. The fatty acid composition of Broccoli seed oil by weight is: palmitic 3.25%, oleic acid 13.5%, linoleic acid 11.4%, linolenic acid (alpha) 9%, eicosenoic 6% and erucic acid 49%.

Carrot Oil
INCI: *Daucus carota*
Carrot oil has regenerating and toning effects, which is excellent for mature and congested skin, psoriasis, eczema, and for sensitive, couperose skin. It contains vitamins B, C, D, and E, minerals, beta carotene and essential fatty acids which is a rich source of vitamin A. It is excellent for sensitive skin. It is reported to tone skin, stimulating elasticity, and reduce scarring. Carrot oil helps to balance the moisture in our skin and conditions hair.

Castor Oil, USP
INCI: *Ricinus communis*
Castor oil, USP is a vegetable oil extracted from the seed of the castor plant. It is used commercially in 50% of lipsticks in the United States. Castor oil creates a protective barrier on the skin and is soothing. It is a triglyceride that is mainly composed of ricinoleic acid (87%), a fatty acid with an unusual molecular structure. Ricinoleic acid is a monounsaturated, 18-carbon fatty acid that has an unusual hydroxyl functional group on the twelfth carbon. It is this

functional group that makes castor oil unusually polar. Castor oil is a colorless to very pale yellow liquid with mild or no odor nor taste.

Castor Oil, Sulfated
INCI: *Ricinus communis*
Castor oil, Sulfated is commonly known as "Turkey Red." It is a sulfated castor oil which is created by adding sulfuric acid to castor oil. The resulting oil is water-soluble. Sulfated castor oil is the only oil that completely disperses in water which makes it an ideal carrier for essential oils in bath oil.

Coconut Oil
INCI: *Cocos nucifera*
Pure coconut oil has a small molecular structure which allows it to be easily absorbed by the skin. It leaves the skin feeling soft and smooth but not oily. Coconut oil is great for the skin because of its antioxidant properties, which gives it a long shelf life. The antioxidants in coconut oil stop the chain reaction of free-radicals creating more free-radicals. Because of the antioxidants, coconut oil not only softens your skin but protects it from further damage, while promoting healthy skin. Coconut oil is also the richest source of good, medium-chain fatty acids, which our sebum also produces as a protective layer on the skin to kill harmful germs.

Coconut oil is vegetable-sourced oil that is naturally free of the need for pesticides and other chemicals to grow and harvest. Some of the myths about coconut oil come from the belief in post-World War II times that coconut contained high levels of cholesterol, which internally or topically would result in acne. Current research on the chemical composition of coconut oil has proven that it does not contain cholesterol at all. Coconut oil contains lauric acid, which actually supports the antibacterial activity of the skin's cells.

Coconut oil is the number-one oil used to make surfactants and castile soap because it produces a nice lather. Coconut in its pure form—when it has not gone through a chemical synthesis with another ingredient—does not dry the skin. Some surfactant-based cleansers that are formulated to strip the skin do leave it feeling dry, and that is wrongly blamed on the coconut. Cleansers that are formulated for oily skin are typically designed to strip away the oily layer on the skin. Many consumers feel that their skin is truly clean in this state. However, the skin produces more oil when it is dry and a vicious cycle of oily, dry, oily, and dry is created. Soaps and cleansers can wash away the protective layer of oil and acid on our skin, leaving it feeling tight and dry. Using a coconut-based moisturizer helps make the skin feel better and helps reestablish the protective layer of oil.

Coconut oil contains the fatty acids caprylic acid, capric acid, and lauric acid. Many of the coconut-derived ingredients can be identified easily by these fatty acids. Coconut oil consists of 90% saturated fat. It is made up mostly of medium-chain triglycerides which are 92% saturated fatty acids (44.6% lauric acid, 16.8% myristic acid, 8.2% palmictic acid, 8% caprylic acid), 6% monounsaturated fatty acids (oleic acid) and 2% polyunsaturated fatty acids (linoleic acid). Coconut melts at 76 degrees Fahrenheit, but if it is stored at a cooler temperature it is solid. Coconut oil resists rancidity because it is slow to oxidize.

Coconut Oil, Fractionated
INCI: *Cocos nucifera* also-known-as *Caprylic/Capric Triglyceride*
Many people are familiar with whole coconut oil which is a solid a room temperature but do not have experience with fractionated coconut oil. But if you haven't tried it you are missing out on a truly great carrier (fixed) oil product.

All carrier oils consist of a class of molecules called fatty acid triglycerides which means they contain three, long-chain fatty ester groups. Most all plant-derived carrier oils consist entirely of what are called "unsaturated" fatty acid triglycerides which means they have one or more carbon-carbon double bonds in their long, fatty, ester side-chains which are typically 16 to 20-plus carbon units long. The double bonds in these side chains are susceptible to oxidation over time, and their reactions with oxygen are what produce the rancid odor you may have noticed in your carrier oils when they get old.

Whole coconut oil also has some quite long unsaturated fatty acid triglycerides (which is why it is a solid at room temperature). But fractionated coconut oil is special in that it has a relatively high percentage of shorter length (C8, C10), completely saturated (no double bonds) triglycerides. These smaller fatty acid triglycerides are separated from the whole coconut oil to give us what is known as "fractionated coconut oil."

The separation process is non-chemical and involves a simple physical separation process, so there are no chemical residues to worry about. Fractionated coconut oil has an indefinite shelf life and is light, non-greasy, non-staining, liquid oil. It is great for use in massage, toiletries, aromatherapy and soap. Fractionated coconut oil is a very good choice for use with essential oils, as it helps carry therapeutic oils under the skin. Fractionated coconut oil can be used in creams, lotions, bath oils, bath salts and soap. Fractionated coconut oil is especially useful in face creams where light oil is desired. It is a good substitute for sweet almond oil if you are concerned about rancidity or a short shelf life. My favorite use for fractionated coconut oil is as a base for massage oil because it does not leave the sheets smelling rancid.

Cranberry Seed Oil

INCI: *Vaccinium macrocarpon*

Cranberry seed oil is essential fatty acid oil recently introduced into the supplement industry. It is the only available oil with a one-to-one ratio of omega-6 (linoleic) to omega-3 (alpha-linolenic) fatty acids. Cranberry seed oil has oxidative stability and contains 70% essential fatty acids making it a superb emollient, lubricant and conditioner for the skin. It is excellent for use in skin, hair, lip, and baby care. Cranberry seed oil contributes to the lipid barrier protection of the skin and assists in moisture retention. The oil also contains high concentrations of tocopherols, tocotrienols, phytosterols, phospholipids, and vitamin A, redefining performance and stability standards for highly polyunsatruated oils.

Evening Primrose

INCI: *Oenothers bennis*

Evening primrose oil is extracted from the seeds of a plant native to North America. However, it grows in Europe and parts of the Southern Hemisphere as well. The evening primrose plant has yellow flowers that bloom only in the evening, hence the name. Each blossom lasts only one day, blooming as the sun sets and withering after the sunrise. It can grow to be up to eight feet tall. Interestingly enough, evening primrose is considered a "weed" in most gardens. However, the oil that it produces is highly valuable both topically and orally.

Evening primrose oil is rich in the essential fatty acids linoleic acid (74%), gamma linoleic acid (9-10%) (GLA) and contains polysaturated omega-6 fatty acids. Evening primrose capsules are commonly taken orally for eczema, breast pain, lowering cholesterol, menopausal symptoms, PMS, osteoporosis and decreasing the risk of heart attack. Evening primrose oil is used topically for acne, eczema and psoriasis; it is the perfect addition to a formula designed to moisturize and soothe damaged skin.

Grapeseed Oil

INCI: *Vitis vinifera*

Grapeseed oil is pressed from the seeds of *Vitis vinifera* grapes, which are typically wine grapes. Since grape seeds are not used in the wine making process, the extraction of the seeds into oil has become profitable byproduct of the wine industry. Grapeseed oil is perfect for formulations that require a light, thin oil that is slightly astringent. It leaves a glossy but not oily film on the skin. Grapeseed oil contains an average of 11% saturated fat, 15% oleic acid, 69% linoleic acid, and less than 1% alpha linolenic acid. It is the lightest of oils, and it is virtually odorless. It is widely used in hypoallergenic natural products because it does not often cause allergic reactions in the highly allergic.

Hazelnut Oil

INCI: *Corylus avellana*

Hazelnut oil is extracted from hazelnuts. It penetrates the skin easily. It has some vitamin E content. Cold pressed hazelnut oil is a wonderful, light, penetrating oil that is slightly astringent making it good oil for acne prone skin. It is high in the essential fatty acids and is soothing and healing to dry irritated skin. Studies have shown that it can filter sunrays and is therefore commonly used in sun care products. A good oil for massage, hair care and cream/lotion formulas.

Hemp Seed Oil

INCI: *Cannabis sativa*

Hemp seed oil is extracted from the seeds of the *Cannabis sativa* plant. To most people *Cannabis sativa* is synonymous with marijuana; the Latin name translates to "useful hemp." Because of this we are often asked if our hemp oil is legal. The oil itself is perfectly legal. There is no tetrahydrocannabinol in the final product of hemp oil.

Hemp contains proteins and high quality fat, and it has a remarkable fatty acid profile. It is high in omega-3 and a 1.7% gamma-linolenic acid. It is 57% linoleic and 19% linoleic acids. This oil has the lowest amount of saturated fatty acids and the highest amount of the polyunsaturated essential fatty acids (linoleic and linolenic acids). Hemp is wonderful oil for dry or mature skin since it is said to help stimulate cell growth.

Hemp seed oil is an emollient. According to the AMA's Committee on Coetaneous Health, emollients help make the skin feel softer and smoother, reduce roughness, cracking and irritation and may possibly retard the fine wrinkles of aging. Hemp seed has a lot of minerals and is good for the skin and hair. Use this in your soaps, lotions and lip balms. It also makes a great lotion bar with almond oil and cocoa butter.

Jojoba Oil

INCI: *Simmondsia chinensis*

Jojoba oil is cold pressed from the nuts of the jojoba tree. The jojoba tree is cultivated in California, Arizona, Mexico, and Israel. Jojoba is pronounced *Ho Ho Ba*. Native Americans have been using jojoba for centuries. The first record of jojoba is from 1701. Father Junipero Serrra found that Native Americans were using Jojoba to treat sores, cuts and burns, and as a conditioner and for all over skin and hair treatments.

Jojoba is technically not oil, but a liquid wax ester with a long unsaturated carbon chain. Chemically it resembles sperm whale oil or spermaceti oil. It was a popular ingredient in creams. The United States banned all sperm whale products in the 1970s because they were contributing to the extinction of sperm whales. In 1977 domestic commercial jojoba oil cultivation began because it is the natural substitute for spermaceti which, in other cases, has been replaced by synthetic products.

Jojoba esters are composed of straight chain alcohols. The acid and the alcohol portions have 20 or 22 carbon atoms and one unsaturated bond. It resembles human sebum, the natural coating our body produces to protect the skin and keeps it supple. Our skin loses sebum with age, sun, wind, cold, and the environment. It contains protein, minerals and a waxy substance that mimics collagen.

Jojoba is perfect skin therapy for any skin type. It has a large molecular structure. Jojoba can help dry or oily skin. If your skin has an over-production of sebum, jojoba oil will dissolve clogged pores and restore the skin to its natural pH balance. The reason jojoba oil works so well that it actually penetrates the skin is because it is accepted as sebum.

Although jojoba oil is very expensive, it does have a long shelf life; it will never break down or go rancid. Jojoba is expensive because it takes 1,200 whole jojoba nuts to add up to a pound which has a 50% yield of oil. Because jojoba has very little scent it works as a wonderful natural perfume base. Jojoba is not greasy and absorbs right into the skin. JMC Technologies has conducted scientific research proving that jojoba can increase skin softness by up to 37%, it reduces superficial lines and wrinkles up to 25% upon application and up to 11% after 8 hours. Jojoba oil is considered to be hypoallergenic oil.

Meadowfoam Seed Oil
INCI: *Limnanthes alba*
One of my favorite oils is meadowfoam seed oil because it is probably the single, most unique oil available on the market today. Meadowfoam seed oil comes from a low-growing herbaceous winter annual that gets its name from the fact that fields of meadowfoam in full bloom appear to look like a meadow of foam. It is native to the Pacific Northwest. Meadowfoam has a good, stable shelf life because it contains over 98% long chain fatty acids. Its unique chemical properties make it one of the most stable of all of the carrier oils.

Refined meadowfoam is virtually odorless which makes it a prime candidate for use in aromatherapy products. It is rich in antioxidants and penetrates the skin easily. The stability of meadowfoam seed oil actually works to extend the shelf life of less stable ingredients in a formula. Meadowfoam is such unique and valuable oil that it is currently being studied by scientists at Oregon State University and the US Department of Agriculture.

When added to cosmetics and creams, meadowfoam re-moisturizes the skin like no other oil. In shampoos and soaps it helps add shine and moisture to the hair and scalp that are otherwise made dry and brittle by the harsh process of daily washing. In lipsticks and balms, it helps revitalize dry, cracked lips, and it helps retain moisture all day long. In many natural formulations, meadowfoam seed oil is often used in place of jojoba oil or sperm whale oil. Its texture, stability and ability to adhere to the skin makes meadowfoam a good candidate to replace castor oil lip formulations.

Meadowfoam oil, when applied to the skin, forms a moisture barrier which prevents moisture loss from the skin. Meadowfoam oil has a non-greasy feeling and soaks immediately into the skin. An added bonus to meadowfoam is that the quality that makes it adhere to the skin also acts as a binder to retain scent longer for aromatherapy-based products. Meadowfoam oil adds a good slip and lubricant value to massage products and will not turn treatment sheets rancid. Meadowfoam has a high molecular weight, but it does not winterize in cold temperatures like jojoba or avocado oils.

The research and development of meadowfoam began in the late 1950s when the United States Department of Agriculture (USDA) was in search for plants that had potential as a renewable source of raw materials for industry. Commercial development began in 1980 on an experimental 35-acre farm-scale operation in Oregon. Meadowfoam has never reached its full potential for use in industry due to the lack of consistent funding which slowed the development of the potential aspects of this unique renewable oil resource. However, the cosmetic industry has fully embraced this fabulous oil due to its unique texture, slip, moisture retention, and shelf life.

Along with the breakthrough of meadowfoam oil came the discovery of three unknown long chain fatty acids. Meadowfoam oil contains over 98% fatty acids with over 20 carbon atoms. The majority of the fatty acid composition of meadowfoam oil comes from C20 (63%), C21 (1 to 16%) and C22 (2 to 17%) fatty acids. Meadowfoam oil is found in the seeds of the plant which contain 20 to 30% oil. The high euric acid content of meadowfoam is most similar to that of rapeseed oil. However rapeseed is slightly more saturated than meadowfoam oil. Much like rapeseed oil, the by-product of meadowfoam oil produces a meal that can be used as a feed source for livestock.

All around, meadowfoam is the definition of a green product. It was developed to replace sperm whale oil in order to protect the species. It is renewable, sustainable, serves multiple industries, and the fields of meadowfoam flowers provide habitat for birds, insects and other creatures that thrive in the fields. It is grown as a rotation crop for grass seed farming which eliminates the need to burn fields in between grass seed planting and gives the farmer an off-season income. Meadowfoam also has less need for fertilizer and pesticides.

Meadowfoam oil is available cold pressed and refined. The refined version is expeller expressed, and it is virtually odorless. It has a pale yellow color. Cold pressed meadowfoam oil has a distinct herbaceous grassy odor and has a dark orange color that comes from the powerful antioxidant known as 3-MBTU, which holds a US Patent. The cold pressed is a virgin triglyceride oil that is clarified using only filtration. It is rich in the delicate active materials such as tocopherols, carotenoids and phystosterol. Use of the cold pressed oil can be problematic due to the strong natural aroma, but with proper formulating it can be used successfully.

Rosehip Seed Oil
INCI: *Rosa mosqueta*
Rosehip seed oil is extracted by cold pressing the seeds of the bright red bud (hip) of a wild rose bush native to Chile. The rosehip seed pod is what is left after the rose petals fall off of a rose. I find that, in nature, nothing is wasted; the power packed oil that comes from rosehips is a great testament to that fact.

Rosehip seed oil has a high content of unsaturated essential fatty acids (80%). It is made up of monounsaturated omega-9 fatty acid oleic acid (15-20%), unsaturated omega-6 fatty acid linoleic acid (44-50%) and linolenic (30-35%). Rosehip seed oil contains bio-available trans-retinoic acid which is highly compatible and easily absorbed into the skin. It also has high vitamin C content.

Rosehip seed oil is highly regarded for the properties it brings to the skin care industry. It is known as a very reparative oil that revitalizes dry, rough, damaged, scarred and dull skin. It is used in the treatment of wrinkles, sun damage, dry skin, scars, and it is restorative for all skin issues. It is quite absorbent and almost instantly hydrates tissue and brings moisture balance to winter skin in arid climates. It is well-known for its use in treatment after radiation. It is also known to accelerate the healing of burns and all known effects of aging including brown spots, wrinkles, and deep lines in the skin. At least one or more of your serious anti-aging and face-oriented products should have this key oil.

Safflower Oil
INCI: *Carthamus tinctorius*
safflower oil comes from the seeds of an herbaceous thistle-like annual flower. Safflower oil is polyunsaturated oil that is similar to sunflower oil in nutritional value and shelf life. Safflower and sunflower are relatively unstable when exposed to high heat, light or oxygen. Both safflower and sunflower are good to use in low-heat or no-heat formulas. Safflower oil contains the monounsaturated omega-9 fatty acid oleic acid (78.9%), unsaturated omega-6 fatty acid linoleic (11%), palmitic acid (6.2%), and linolenic (.02%).

Sunflower Oil
INCI: *Helianthus annuus*
Sunflower oil is extracted from the seeds of the sunflower. It is made up of predominately linoleic acid (48-74%), monounsaturated omega-9 fatty acid oleic acid (14-40%), palmitic acid (4-9%) and stearic acid (1-7%). There are several versions of sunflower produced, ranging from high linoleic, high oleic and mid oleic. The variations in the unsaturated fatty acid profile are factors of both the growing climate and genetics of the plant. All sunflower oil has high vitamin E content.

Sunflower oil is used primarily in the food industry but has applications in the cosmetic industry as well. It helps form a seal that retains moisture yet allows the skin to breathe. An interesting study found that sunflower oil used as a treatment for low birth weight pre-term infants lowered the rate of infections by 41 percent. The theory is that pre-mature babies have underdeveloped skin which leaves them more susceptible to infections and that sunflower oil created the much needed barrier on the skin.

Tamanu Oil
INCI: *Calophyllum inophyllum*
Tamanu oil, also known as Foraha oil in Africa, is obtained by mechanically crushing the dried nuts of the Tamanu tree. The Tamanu tree is typically found in the Pacific and Asian Tropical regions. The oil is rich and deep in color, and it smells similar to butter pecan ice cream. Tamanu oil has a soothing effect on the skin, and it helps to relieve irritations such as sun burn, inflammation and general rashes. Tamanu oil also helps regenerate skin cells and has a hydrating effect on the skin.

Research shows that Tamanu oil is a strong anti-inflammatory, making it useful for the treatment of rheumatism, eczema and inflammatory skin conditions. The oil has been used for its ability to help heal cuts and wounds while acting as a germicide to prevent infection. Use tamanu oil undiluted as a treatment for eczema, psoriasis, cuts and wounds or in creams and lotions for general treatment of dry skin. Tamanu oil can also be healing in lip balms and lotion bars at 5%.

Opinion of Mineral Oil and Petroleum
Mineral oil and petroleum are the by-products of the distillation of petroleum in the manufacturing of gasoline. Both are very commonly found in your cosmetics. Take a moment and check the ingredient deck of what you have around the house.

Petroleum jelly interrupts your own skin's ability to moisturize itself. Petroleum jelly is often used to correct dry skin, but in fact it creates more problems by interfering in the natural cycle of the skin which leads to excessive dryness and chapping. It creates a vicious cycle of dryness. Breaking the cycle will create only a few days of dry skin until your skin can rebound.

My opinion is that soda pop is to water what petroleum is to plant butters. Soda pop is full of empty calories and often, caffeine, and this creates a long-term dependence on the drink. Water hydrates and restores the body. Petroleum offers nothing of value to the skin and comes up empty every time in addition to creating a long term addiction. Plant butters are rich, soothing, and feed the skin, allowing it to restore itself. Petroleum used for dry skin creates more dry skin which creates a vicious cycle. Plant butters nourish dry skin and work synergistically with the natural process of the skin.

While many soda pops often include naturally sourced ingredients, petroleum is a byproduct of drilling for petroleum, which is then further refined. Just like many soda pops the natural origins of petroleum are lost in its ill effects on the body. The refining process of petroleum also makes it unappealing to vegans due to the fact that is processed and filtered through bone-char.

Waxes

Beeswax
INCI: Beeswax
Beeswax is a natural wax that comes from the honeycomb of virgin bees. Bees process honey form the nectar and then convert it into wax. Ten pounds of honey produces one pound of wax. It has a honey like fragrance. Beeswax is commonly used in balms, salves and ointments. Beeswax is insoluble in water which does not make it an ideal emulsifier in lotions and crèmes. It has a high melting point. Beeswax is available in yellow and white prills at Essential Wholesale. It can also be purchased in solid blocks. The use of beeswax disqualifies a product as a vegan certified product.

Candelilla Wax
INCI: *Euphorbia antisyphillitica/ped*
Candelilla wax is taken from the candelilla plant a desert shrub that is native to Mexico and Texas. It is used as a thickener in balms, salves, ointments and butters. It can be used in the same proportions in a recipe as beeswax. The Candelilla plant (meaning "little candle") forms in clusters of thin, straight, wax covered stems along rock ledges. The plant is harvested to extract the thick waxy coating. Candelilla wax consists of mainly hydrocarbons, esters of higher molecular weight, free acids, and resins. It is insoluble in water.

Carnauba Wax

INCI: *Copernica cerifera*

Carnauba Wax is a natural product obtained from the processing of the powder exuded from the leaves of the palm tree. The carnauba palm tree protects itself against dehydration during the periods of drought that severely affects the Northeast region of Brazil every year for more than six months. The plant covers its leaves with a thick layer of wax consisting basically of esters, alcohols and fatty acids of high molecular weight. Once the leaves have been collected, they are dried out and beaten for the wax to loosen up. After going through a refining process that includes filtering, distillation, centrifugation and natural bleaching, the wax is used all over the world by various industries, such as in the manufacture of polishing wax (floors, shoes, cars etc.), in the paper and packaging industries, in making paints and other more resistant continuous coatings, in the cosmetic industry (lipsticks, enamels), in the food industry (bubble gum, chocolate, fruits), as well as in the pharmaceutical industry.

Cosmetic Chemicals

Carbomer

Carbomer is a water soluble thickener, suspending agent and stabilizer often used in cosmetics. Carbomer is a synthetic high molecular weight cross-linked polymers of acrylic acid. It has excellent thickening efficiency at high viscosity and sparkling clear transparency in aqueous solutions. Carbomer is a high molecular weight polymer. It is not absorbed by body tissues and is totally safe for human oral consumption. Test for toxicological tolerance have shown that it does not have pronounced physiological action and is non -toxic. Carbomer is used in conjunction with TEA to adjust the pH and thicken the product to a stable viscosity.

Dipropylene Glycol

Dipropylene glycol is produced as a byproduct of the manufacture of propylene glycol. It works well as a solvent of essential and fragrance oils. Dipropylene glycol is not acutely toxic by oral, dermal, or inhalation exposure. Dipropylene glycol is not toxic to genetic material based on in vitro and in vivo study findings. Dipropylene glycols low toxicity and solvent properties make it an ideal additive for perfumes, reed diffusers and skin and hair care products. It is also a common ingredient in commercial fog fluid used in entertainment industry smoke and haze machines.

Polysorbate 20

Polysorbate 20 is a non-ionic surfactant that is used to disperse and emulsify oils into water. It is an indispensable oil-dispersant in body mists and spritzers. Polysorbate 20 is made from lauric acid (olive oil source) connected to a sugar (sorbitol) and this compound is then ethoxylated (grain based alcohol) to make it water dispersible. It is non-irritating. It is critical that an emulsifier used with essential is nonionic, because it does not disrupt the properties of the essential oils by creating ionic bonds which are formed when two or more atoms give up electrons. A nonionic bond does not borrow electrons is preferable when using essential oils. Ionic bonds are stronger and do not separate in solution, but they do disrupt the properties of the essential oils. For this reason I recommend Polysorbate 20 over any other emulsifier on the market.

As you know oil and water don't mix, but in cosmetic chemistry the solution to blending two immiscible (unblendable) liquids are emulsions. Oil simply can't form a strong bond with water on its own. Emulsifiers work by forming a sort of skin around small droplets of oil which allows the oil droplets to remain suspended in a solution of water in an oil-in-water (O/W) formula. The opposite is true in a water-in-oil (W/O) solution. Emulsifiers have a large lipophilic end (attracted to oil) and a hydrophilic end (attracted to water). These lipophilic and hydrophilic ends create a game of tug-of-war between the oil and water which keeps the oil suspended in a water solution.

Triethanolamine
Triethanolamine (TEA) is a clear, viscous liquid used to reduce the surface tension in emulsions. This allows the water-soluble and oil-soluble ingredients in a formula to blend better. It is a strong base, which makes it useful in adjusting the pH of a cosmetic formula. TEA is completely soluble in water and is rapidly biodegradable.

TEA neutralizes fatty acids and solubilizes oils and other ingredients that are not completely soluble in water. TEA combines the properties of both amines and alcohols and can undergo reactions common to both groups. As an amine, TEA reacts with acids because it is mildly alkaline, and forms soaps. When TEA acts as an alcohol it is hygroscopic and can cause the esterification of free fatty acids.

The FDA includes TEA on its list of indirect food additives, which means TEA may be used in adhesives in contact with food and to assist in the washing or peeling of fruits and vegetables. The safety of TEA has been assessed by the CIR Expert Panel which concluded that TEA is safe for use in cosmetics and personal care products designed for discontinuous, brief use followed by thorough rinsing from the surface of the skin. In products intended for prolonged contact with the skin, the concentration of TEA should not exceed 5%.

Alpha Hydroxy Acids

Alpha hydroxy acids (AHA) are any of various carboxylic acids with a hydroxyl group attached at the alpha position. Examples include: malic, lactic, glycolic, citric and tartaric acid. AHA's are used in cosmetics for its exfoliating effect on the surface layer of skin. The FDA requires that you include this warning on any product made with AHAs: Sunburn Alert: This product contains an alpha hydroxy acid (AHA) that may increase your skin's sensitivity to the sun and particularly the possibility of sunburn. Use a sunscreen and limit sun exposure while using this product and for a week afterwards.

Citric Acid is commonly used in hair and skincare products. It has astringent and antioxidant properties and can also be used as a stabilizer and preservative, and to neutralize odor. It is derived from citrus fruits by fermentation of crude sugars. It is used to adjust acid-alkali balance. When citric acid is used to adjust the pH of a cosmetic product the FDA does not require that it be included on the ingredient list.

Glycolic Acid is a constituent of sugar cane juice. Glycolic acid is form of an alpha hydroxy acid that is extremely strong and must be handled with extreme care. Please be cautious in your formulations that contain glycolic acid. It is not necessary to use large percentages of glycolic acid in order to have a positive effect on the skin.

While the FDA does allow the use of 10% in "at home" products, I advise that you experiment with percentage ranges of 1-5% in your formulations. We have found that smaller percentages used more often can be more effective and less traumatic to the skin than high doses used irregularly. Recovery time should be a matter of hours and not days or weeks as with some glycolic acid products on the market.

According to the FDA, "the panel concluded that AHA's are 'safe for use in cosmetic products at concentrations less than or equal to 10 percent, at final formulation pH's greater than or equal to 3.5, when formulated to avoid increasing the skin's sensitivity to the sun, or when directions for use include the daily use of sun protection.' For salon use products, the panel said that the products are 'safe for use at concentrations less than or equal to 30 percent, at final formulation pH's greater than or equal to 3.0, in products designed for brief, discontinuous use followed by thorough rinsing from the skin, when applied by trained professionals, and when application is accompanied by directions for the daily use of sun protection.'"

Lactic Acid, also known as milk acid, is an alpha hydroxy acid that is derived from sour or fermented milk. Cleopatra is often cited as having bathed in milk, but the reality is that it was sour milk.

Malic acid is an alpha hydroxy fruit acid, can be used in skin care products to rejuvenate and improve skin conditions. Malic acid is a natural constituent of many fruits and vegetables that are preserved by fermentation. This acid may be broken down during fermentation by certain bacteria into lactic acid and carbon dioxide.

Multiple Fruit Blend Tincture is a hydro-alcohol mixture prepared from organic plant materials (lemon, orange, cane sugar, maple, bilberry, cranberry), organic alcohol and de-ionized water. The Multiple Fruit Acids Tincture contains naturally occurring alpha hydroxy acids (AHA's). The AHA's are water soluble components of the Multiple Fruits which maximized the stimulation of cell renewal while minimizing irritation associated with the use of topical alpha hydroxy acids.

Tartaric Acid is an organic alpha hydroxy acid found in many plants and known to the early Greeks and Romans as tartar, the acid potassium salt derived as a deposit from fermented grape juice.

Additives

Alpha Hydroxy Liquid Bundle
INCI: Vegetable Glycerin, Malic Acid, Tartaric Acid, Citric Acid, Glycolic Acid, Lactose

This bundle is a blend of glycolic crystals, milk sugar and other fruit acids to help skin appear smoother, softer, and tighter. While the FDA does allow the use of 10% in "at home" products, the manufacturer Essential Wholesale advises that you experiment with percentage ranges of 1-5% in your formulations.

According to the FDA, "the panel concluded that AHA's are 'safe for use in cosmetic products at concentrations less than or equal to 10 percent, at final formulation pH's greater than or equal to 3.5, when formulated to avoid increasing the skin's sensitivity to the sun, or when directions for use include the daily use of sun protection.' For salon use products, the panel said that the products are 'safe for use at concentrations less than or equal to 30 percent, at final formulation pH's greater than or equal to 3.0, in products designed for brief, discontinuous use followed by thorough rinsing from the skin, when applied by trained professionals, and when application is accompanied by directions for the daily use of sun protection.'"

Castile Soap
Castile Soap was originally 100% olive oil soap. It got its name from the Castile

region in Spain. It is extremely mild, liquid with water like consistency. It always has a pH of 9 or above.

Glycerin, Vegetable
INCI: Glycerin
Kosher Vegetable Glycerin, also referred to as Glycerol, is a sugar alcohol that is obtained by adding alkali to fats and fixed oils. Glycerin is a soothing humectant that draws moisture from the air to the skin. It is an emollient, which makes the skin feel softer and smoother. Glycerin has a high hydrophilic (water) factor and a low lipophilic (fat) factor. It is completely miscible with water. The FDA includes Glycerin on its list of direct food additives considered Generally Recognized As Safe (GRAS), and on its list of approved indirect food additives. According to the general provisions of the Cosmetics Directive of the European Union, Glycerin may be used in cosmetics and personal care products marketed in Europe. Glycerin derived from raw materials of animal origin must comply with European Union animal by-products regulations. The Joint FAO/WHO Expert Committee on Food Additives has not specified an acceptable daily intake for Glycerin. Glycerol is considered to be readily biodegradable in the aquatic environment.

Hyaluronic Acid
INCI: Sodium Hyaluronate
Hyaluronic Acid was discovered by Karl Meyer in 1934 and has been successfully used in personal care and wound healing. Until the 1990's the only method of producing hyaluronic acid was extracting it from rooster combs. Currently there are two forms of hyaluronic acid on the market; one derived from rooster comb and the other derived by the fermentation of yeast. I only recommend the 100% vegan approved material.

Hyaluronic acid is naturally found in the extracellular matrix of human tissue. Topically applied hyaluronic acid forms an air permeable layer and penetrates into the dermis, thus boosting the elasticity and hydration of the skin. The protective breathable barrier on the skin locks in moisture which gives the skin a youthful appearance. The cuticular layer of the skin normally contains 10-20% water, however as we age it can drop to below 10%. Hyaluronic acid comes to the rescue with its unique ability to hold more than 1000 ml of water per gram of hyaluronic acid, which is a key factor in allowing the skin to retain more water. Amazingly, hyaluronic acid adjusts its moisture absorption based on the relative humidity in the air. It is the ideal ingredient in skin care products as it adjusts to the skin's need for a moisturizing effect depending on the relative humidity of seasons and climate of an area. Hyaluronic acid also protects the epidermis by scavenging reactive oxygen species generated by ultra violet light which would normally cause sunspots.

Hydrogen Peroxide

Hydrogen peroxide is commercially available in 33-37% solutions, but is most commonly found in your local drug store at 3% solution. The recipes in this book call for the 3% stabilized pharmaceutical grade hydrogen peroxide that you find at your local store. Hydrogen peroxide is H_2O_2, which means that it has just one more atom of oxygen then water (H_2O) does. The recipes in this book use hydrogen peroxide in household products only to cleanse, disinfect and whiten.

Lavender Distillate

INCI: *Lavendula angustifolia*

Distillate, also known as hydrosols are commonly sold under the terms distillate waters, hydrosols, hydrolates, hydrolats, plant waters and floral waters. They are the aromatic by-product created during the steam distillation of plant material in the manufacturing of essential oils. The hydrosols are the condensed water collected in the process of steam distillation. While hydrosols are aromatic in nature their aroma is very subtle. Lavender distillate is readily available and abundant.

Neem Tincture/Extract

INCI: *Azadirachta Indica*

Neem tincture is under-utilized in the Western culture. In India neem is very popular and commonly used as an antibacterial, antiviral, antifungal, antiseptic, anti-parasitic agent in toiletries, soap, toothpaste and skin/hair care products.

Rosin

Rosin is brittle and friable, with a faint piney odor and has a glassy solid that easily crystalizes when brought into solution. The practical melting point is 210°F to 248°F. It is very flammable, burning with a smoky flame, so care should be taken when melting it. It is soluble in alcohol, ether, benzene and chloroform. Rosin consists mainly of abietic acid, and combines with caustic alkalis to form salts that are known as rosin soaps. Rosin is extensively used in soap making and wax hair removal products.

Vitamin E

INCI: Tocopherol

Vitamin E is widely used in massage oils, balms, ointments, salves and cosmetics as an antioxidant to the oils in the formula. I5t is obtained by the vacuum distillation of vegetable oils.

White Vinegar
INCI: Acetic Acid
Vinegar is produced through fermentation of ethanol by acetic acid bacteria. White vinegar is often used as a household cleaner. Its acidic nature allows it to easily dissolve mineral deposits and works as an effective solvent. A Good Housekeeping study found that a 5% vinegar solution is 90% effective against mold and 99.9% effective against bacteria. It also works as an effective softener in laundry products.

Witch Hazel USP
INCI: *Hamamelis Virginiana*
This is a very common ingredient in various cosmetics and is used as a local anesthetic and astringent. It is made from the twigs and leaves of *Hamamelis Virginiana*. Witch hazel USP contains 14% ethyl alcohol.

Surfactants

Surfactants are a vehicle used in cosmetic chemistry. They are important building blocks in personal care products. Surfactants allow cosmetics to slip across, onto or to clean the skin by breaking up and separating from the skin oils, fats, makeup, dirt, pollution and other debris.

There are four basic types of surfactants used in cosmetics.

- Anionic surfactants have a negative ionic charge. (Sodium Laureth Sulfate, Sodium Lauryl Sulfate, Stearic Acid,)
- Cationic surfactants have a positive ionic charge. (Cetearyl Alcohol, Stearalkonium Chloride)
- Amphoteric surfactants may have either a positive or negative ionic charge. Amphoeteric surfactants adapt to the pH of the water used in the formula. (Cocamidopropyl betaine, Sodium-Cocoamphoacetate)
- Nonionic surfactants have no charge. (Decyl Glucoside, Polysorbate)

Surfactants by definition lower the surface tension of the skin and/or of the water in a formula. Surfactants are both hydrophilic (water loving) and lipophilic (oil loving) which gives them the ability to reduce surface tension in a water and oil formula. Surfactants are commonly used in products that are designed to cleanse (shampoo, shower gel, face cleanser, hand soap), emulsify water and oil (lotion, crème), solubilize (polysorbate solubizing essential oil into a toner, body mist) or condition (hair conditioner).

Bio-Terge 804 has the INCI name: Sodium C14-16 Olefin Sulfonate, Sodium Laureth Sulfate, and Lauramide DEA. Below is a closer look at the ingredients that make up Bio-Terge 804.

Cocoamidopropyl Betaine is a fairly mild and gentle surfactant used in melt and pour soaps, shampoos, conditioners, and body washes. It has been valued for its foaming qualities and, ability to serve as a thickening agent. Cocoamidopropyl betaine leaves hair and skin soft and smooth. It is compatible with other cationic, anionic, and nonionic surfactants making it a favorite of cosmetic formulators. Cocamidopropyl betaine has an exceptional safety profile and performs markedly well.

Cocamidopropyl betaine is a long chain surfactant derived from coconut oil. Skeptics are alarmed by the fact that during the synthesis of this ingredient, some of the reagents involved in the reaction may be potentially harmful. A solid comprehension of the chemistry involved in reagents will help clarify this debate. A reagent is a substance that is used in a chemical reaction to produce other substances. It is not in the final product. An example of this could be the Sodium Hydroxide when it is used to cause a reaction called saponification to create soap. Sodium Hydroxide is an ingredient with multiple hazard warnings, but when combined with other constituents it creates an effective, safe, and diverse cleaning agent. There is no un-reacted sodium hydroxide in the finished soap because a new product has been formed.

The Cosmetic Ingredient Review (CIR) Expert Panel reviewed Cocamidopropyl betaine and found it to be safe for use as used in rinse of products and limited it to 3% for leave-on products. According to the general provisions of the Cosmetics Directive of the European Union, Cocamidopropyl betaine may be used in cosmetics and personal care products marketed in Europe. In tests Cocoamidopropyl betaine was found to be readily biodegradable, slightly orally toxic, moderately irritating to the eyes, mildly irritating to the skin, and no delayed contact hypersensitivity or evidence of sensitization was observed. It is not a mutagenic, nor is it a carcinogen

Lauramide DEA (from Bio-Terge surfactant blend) is a fatty acid derivative of diethanolamine (DEA*). It is a nonionic surfactant used in the formulation of shampoos, hair dyes, bath products and lotions as a viscosity booster and, to increase and stabilize the foaming capacity of a formula. Lauramide DEA also thickens the aqueous portion of a formula. Lauramide DEA is produced from naturally occurring lauric acid.

The CIR Expert Panel concluded that Lauramide DEA was safe as a cosmetic ingredient. The CIR Expert Panel reviewed data on Lauramide DEA showing that: it is slightly toxic to non-toxic via acute oral administration; it is not a dermal toxin in acute and sub-chronic studies; it is a mild skin irritant but not a sensitizer or photosensitizer; it is a mild to moderate eye irritant; it does not demonstrate mutagenic activity.

Lauramide DEA is listed under Fatty Acid Dialkylamides and Dialkanolamides in the Cosmetics Directive of the European Union (see Annex III, Part I) and may be used with a maximum secondary amine concentration of 0.5%. It may not be used with nitrosating systems. In the Cosmetics Directive of the European Union, Lauramide DEA was lumped into the Fatty Acid Dialkylamides and Dialkanolamides along with Cocamide DEA, Linoleamide DEA and Oleamide DEA. The CIR Expert Panel determined that only Cocamide DEA should not be used with nitrosating systems.

*Since Lauramide DEA is a fatty acid derivative of diethanolamine (DEA) I wanted to take a moment to address the safety data regarding DEA. DEA has been assessed by the CIR Expert Panel and concluded they that DEA is safe for use in cosmetics and personal care products designed for discontinuous, brief use followed by thorough rinsing from the surface of the skin. In products intended for prolonged contact with the skin, the concentration of DEA should not exceed 5%.

Sodium C14-16 Olefin Sulfonate (a Sodium Alpha-Olefin Sulfonate) is a mixture of long chain sulfonate salts prepared by the sulfonation of alpha olefins. The numbers (14-16) indicate the average lengths of the carbon chains of the alpha olefins. It is most commonly used in shampoos and bath and shower products. Sodium C14-16 Olefin Sulfonate helps clean the skin and hair by helping the water from your shower or bath to mix with the oil and dirt on your body and hair so they can be rinsed away.

The FDA reviewed the safety of Sodium C14-16 Olefin Sulfonate as indirect food additives, as components of adhesives, and as emulsifiers and/or surface-active agents. The safety of Sodium C14-16 Olefin Sulfonate has been assessed by the CIR Expert Panel and they concluded that it was safe as used in rinse-off products and safe up to 2% in leave-on products.

The CIR Expert Panel noted that Sodium Alpha-Olefin Sulfonates are poorly absorbed through normal skin but significantly absorbed through damaged skin. Short-term toxicity studies showed no consistent effects. High concentrations produced moderate to mild ocular irritation. At doses that were maternally toxic they found fetal abnormalities in animal studies. Genotoxicity, oral and dermal studies were negative.

Some studies found irritation and sensitization. This sensitization was attributed to low level gamma sultone residues. Because gamma sultones were sensitizers at very low levels, it was concluded that any product containing Sodium Alpha-Olefin Sulfonates should have very little gamma sultone residues. The gamma sultone levels should not exceed 10 ppm for saturated (alkane) sultones, 1 ppm for chlorosultones, and 0.1 ppm for unsaturated sultones. Sodium Alpha-Olefin Sulfonates are otherwise considered safe for use in rinse-off products. The use of Sodium Alpha-Olefin Sulfonates in leave-on products is limited to 2% in a formula. According to the general provisions of the Cosmetics Directive of the European Union, Sodium C14-16 Olefin Sulfonate may be used in cosmetics and personal care products marketed in Europe.

Sodium Laureth Sulfate (SLES) is a very effective cleansing agent that belongs to the chemical class of alkyl ether sulfates. It is a salt of sulfated ethoxylated fatty alcohol and is the most commonly used of the alkyl ether sulfates that are used in cleansing products, including bubble baths, bath soaps and detergents and shampoos.

SLES exhibits emulsifying properties and imparts "softness" to the skin. As a cleansing agent the anionic surfactant SLES wets body surfaces, emulsifies or solubilize oils and suspends soil. It also contributes to the lathering properties and excellent viscosity response in cleansing products and bubble baths formulas. Sodium Laureth Sulfate exhibits a high degree of foaming. SLES was formulated to improved mildness over Sodium Lauryl Sulfate (SLS).

The safety of SLES was assessed in 1983 and re-reviewed in 2002 by the CIR Expert Panel and they concluded SLES is safe for use in cosmetics and personal care products in the present practices of use and concentration when formulated to be non-irritating. It can cause mild to moderate skin irritation in some people.

According to the general provisions of the Cosmetics Directive of the European Union, Sodium Laureth Sulfate may be used in cosmetics and personal care products that are marketed in Europe. SLES did not result in adverse effects in numerous safety studies including acute, sub-chronic and chronic oral exposure, reproductive and developmental toxicity, carcinogenic, photosensitization studies and SLES readily biodegrades.

Despite internet rumors SLES is not a carcinogenic substance. The World Health Organization, the International Agency for the Research of Cancer, US Environment Protection Agency and the European Union are all organizations that classify and register all substances that are known to be carcinogenic. None of these organizations have classified SLES as a carcinogen.

Sodium Lauryl Sulfoacetate: From a chemical standpoint, sodium lauryl sulfoacetate is a very unique surfactant. It demonstrates outstanding performance in cleansing, foaming, wetting, viscosity building, mildness and emulsification. It is an excellent surfactant for any water hardness and is biodegradable making it a versatile ingredient in cosmetic formulation.

Sodium lauryl sulfoacetate was specifically developed to be mild to the skin. It is commonly the surfactant of choice for formulators developing products that are designed for those who have sensitivity to other soaps. The sodium lauryl sulfoacetate molecule is a valuable and unique molecule that has been in use for over 30 years in cosmetics.

Some common characteristics of sodium lauryl sulfoacetate are that it is relatively non-hygroscopic (it does not absorb or retain moisture from the air) and is resistant to hydrolysis (it does not react with water to produce other compounds) even at high temperatures. It is especially stable at the common cosmetic pH range of 5.5 to 7.8. Sodium lauryl sulfoacetate is biodegradable and has shown in laboratory studies to undergo both primary and ultimate biodegradation. This product has a good toxicological profile which makes it an ingredient of choice for dentifrice (toothpastes), shampoos, cleansing creams, sensitive skin soap bars and shower gels. To add to its track record, sodium lauryl sulfoacetate is registered in the United States, Japan, Canada, and Australia and is compliant with the EU regulations.

The safety and mildness of sodium lauryl sulfoacetate is in the absence of a sulfate ion head, which is commonly found in many other surfactants. The sulfate ion, which originates in sulfuric acid, is replaced with the more stable sulfonated ester. This sulfate free surfactant is made with lauryl alcohol, derived from palm kernel oil, which is then condensed with a sulfonated form of acetic acid, or vinegar. It is this charged sulfonated acetate group which gives this molecule its mild surfactant properties.

Fig. 1) Sodium lauryl sulfoacetate

Fig. 2) Sodium lauryl sulfate

Note: in figure 1 and 2 that the molecules posses an identical charge on their head and contain an equal number of carbon atoms attached to their functional group, making them very similar in physical appearance and overall function. The sodium lauryl sulfoacetate however, lacks the potentially harmful sulfate head attached to the carbon chain.

pH Adjusters

Citric Acid
Citric Acid is commonly used in hair and skincare products to lower the pH. It is used to adjust acid-alkali balance. When citric acid is used to adjust the pH of a cosmetic product the FDA does not require that it be included on the ingredient list. Citric acid is not, in and of itself, a preservative, however

because many preservatives are pH dependent it is often mistaken as a preservative.

Sodium Bicarbonate
Sodium Bicarbonate can be used to raise the pH of a finished product. You must be certain that your product does not already contain citric acid or vinegar because the addition of sodium bicarbonate will create an impressive reaction within your product.

Sodium Hydroxide
Sodium Hydroxide is often dissolved in solution to use as a pH adjuster to cosmetics to raise the pH of the finished product. I never use it to adjust pH, but only added it here so that you may recognize why you see it listed in some leave on products.

Colorants and Micas

D&C, FD&C and Lakes
D&C is the abbreviation used with colorants for drug and cosmetics. Colors are monitored by the FDA. "Under the Federal Food, Drug, and Cosmetic Act, color additives, except for coal tar hair dyes, are subject to FDA approval before they may be used in food, drugs, or cosmetics, or in medical devices that come in contact with the bodies of people or animals for a significant period of time. The following resources are related to the use of color additives in FDA-regulated products." A colorant with D&C has been approved for use in drugs and cosmetics.

D&C in the name of the color means that this color has been approved for human use by the FDA in Drugs and Cosmetics. All D&C colors are subject to batch certification. This means, "Color additives listed in 21 CFR Parts 74 and 82 must be analyzed and batch certified by FDA before they can be used in any FDA-regulated product marketed in the U.S." (Source FDA)

D&C Orange No. 5 is an orange stain permanently listed for external applied drugs and cosmetics in 1984. This color is a U.S. Certified Organic Colorant which means that this colorant is produced in accordance with U.S. Government specifications, and is certified for use in accordance with the Federal Food, Drug and Cosmetic Act.

D&C Red No 27 is an acid derived from fluorescein (a brilliant red, crystalline dye) and was permanently listed for cosmetic coloring in 1982. This color is a U.S. Certified Organic Colorant which means that this colorant is produced in accordance with U.S. Government specifications, and is certified for use in accordance with the Federal Food, Drug and Cosmetic Act.

D&C Red No. 7 is permanently listed in 1987 for ingested drug and cosmetic lip products and for general cosmetic uses according to good manufacturing practices. This color is a U.S. Certified Organic Colorant which means that this colorant is produced in accordance with U.S. Government specifications, and is certified for use in accordance with the Federal Food, Drug and Cosmetic Act.

D&C Yellow No. 5 is an insoluble Pigment is permanently listed as a color additive since 1966 and rated by the World Health Organization as a 1A, completely safe and acceptable for all nonfood use. This color is a U.S. Certified Organic Colorant which means that this colorant is produced in accordance with U.S. Government specifications, and is certified for use in accordance with the Federal Food, Drug and Cosmetic Act.

FD&C in the name of the color means that this color has been approved for human use by the FDA in Food, Drugs and Cosmetics. All FD&C colors are subject to batch certification. This means, "Color additives listed in 21 CFR Parts 74 and 82 must be analyzed and batch certified by FDA before they can be used in any FDA-regulated product marketed in the U.S." (Source FDA)

FD&C Blue No.1, FD&C Red 40 and FD&C Yellow 5 are dyes certified by the FDA as safe for use in Food, Drugs and Cosmetics and rated by the World Health Organization as a 1A, completely safe and acceptable for all nonfood use. These colors are U.S. Certified Organic Colorants which means that these colorants are produced in accordance with U.S. Government specifications, and are certified for use in accordance with the Federal Food, Drug and Cosmetic Act.

Lakes consist of an organic straight color extended with an inorganic substrate, which makes them insoluble. They are used in oil-based formulas such as lipsticks and lip stains. Since Lakes are insoluble they do not react with other ingredients and the color remains stable even in high heat, pH changes and any viscosity of product. Even though Lakes are insoluble they are miscible in oil and water creates a dispersion of color. Lakes are perfect for non-bleeding lip stains and when it is necessary to not have your colors bleed into one another.

Oxides, Marines and Micas
Bismuth Oxychloride was permanently listed on the Color Additives Approved for use in Cosmetics list by the FDA in 1977. It is a fine powder with a bright luster. It is used in cosmetics because of the pearlescent white color that adds brightness and luster to a color blend. It offers a smooth texture that allows for easy application of a finished color cosmetic.

Carmine is a crimson pigment that is derived from some scale insects. Carmine is commonly used to color cosmetics, apple sauce, yogurt, juice and other foods. It was permanently listed by the FDA for use in food in 1977. Not permitted in vegan certified cosmetics.

Chromium Oxide Green was permanently listed on the Color Additives Approved for use in Cosmetics list by the FDA in 1977. Iron oxides are non-toxic inorganic pigments from iron combined with oxygen. Iron oxides are insoluble and will not bleed into other colors.

Ferric Ferrocyanide, iron blue, is a coloring for cosmetics. It is approved for around the eyes. It was permanently listed by the FDA in 1978 as a color.

Iron Oxides are widely used in cosmetics. They were permanently listed on the Color Additives Approved for use in Cosmetics list by the FDA in 1977. Iron oxides are non-toxic inorganic pigments from iron combined with oxygen. Iron oxides are insoluble and will not bleed into other colors.

Micas are a naturally occurring group of silicate minerals safe for use to formulate cosmetics and personal care products applied to the lips, face and eye area.

Tin Oxide is a coloring ingredient that is used primarily as an opacifier in cosmetics.

Titanium Dioxide is a naturally occurring oxide of titanium. It is used as a white pigment. It is bright and has a high refractive index.

Ultra Marines were permanently listed on the Color Additives Approved for use in Cosmetics list by the FDA in 1976. It is a non-toxic inorganic pigment consisting of silicate of aluminum, sodium and Sulfides or sulfates. Ultramarines are insoluble but miscible in water and oil.

Bulk Bases

A Word about Water Activity and Using Bulk Bases Recipes
You will find this book sprinkled with recipes, however you may notice that there are no recipes provided that contain high water activity such as lotions, crèmes, serums and so forth. Let me explain: You see, it has everything to do with preservation of products for the prevention of bacteria. Bacteria are a fact of life for cosmetics, foods, and pretty much any organism that contains even a trace amount of water.

David Steinberg has trademarked the perfect saying when it comes to bacteria, "Remember, Preservatives are Safer than Bacteria™" Believe it or not, every cosmetic that doesn't use a broad spectrum preservative and contains water has a three-day shelf life, even if it is refrigerated and/or contains essential oils. I know this because I have run extensive tests on products on the market with those claims and tested every form of "natural preservation" out there. If a cosmetic has even a trace amount of water it must be preserved by some method. There is no such thing as a SAFE preservative-free cosmetic.

Cosmetic products containing water must be preserved for two main reasons: insurance companies would never cover unpreserved products and the FDA requires that products are not "injurious to user under conditions of customary use because it contains, or its container is composed of, a potentially harmful substance" and they may not "contain filth." Products are not required to be sterile but they may not be contaminated with a pathogen. All other counts must remain low and remain that way under foreseeable consumer use. The products must be tested for adequacy of preservation during the development of the product and each batch tested before released for sale. While you might have a testing facility in your business, the majority of my readers will not.

Bacteria are very dangerous things; it's illegal in your products, and it's a business killer if it crops up in your cosmetics. Unpreserved or improperly preserved cosmetics are a breeding ground for fungi, yeast, and molds because they prefer acid conditions (pH 5.5-6) at room temperature to multiply.

Determining the water activity of your product is the shortcut to deciding if you need a preservative or not. If your product is bone dry with no water then it does not need a preservative. Bacteria require water to grow and the majority of cosmetics contain high enough water levels to easily grow bacteria. Simply put, bacteria require water to support life, and if you have enough water it will thrive. That is why you will find that recipes I share with you do not contain water or do not require preservation.

Scenting Chart for Bases
Whether you create your own bases, buy them from another supplier or use Essential Wholesale bulk bases this chart will come in handy for you.

Essential Oil Scenting Guide	
Up to 40%	
Reed Diffusers	40%
Perfume	20%-40%
Up to 30%	
Eau de parfum	10-30%
Up to 20%	
Eau de toilette	5-20%

Essential Oil Scenting Guide	
Up to 5%	
Eau de cologne	2-5%
Massage & Body Oil	0.5%-5%
Balm/Ointment/Salve	0.5%-5%
Shower Fizz Tabs	3%-5%
Room Sprays	1%-5%
Up to 3%	
CP Soap	3%
Oil/Butter Body Scrubs	1% - 3%
Body Butters	0.5% - 3%
Lip Balm	0.5% - 3%
Lotion & Creme	0.25% - 3%
Body Mist	1% - 3%
Up to 2%	
Hair Conditioner	0.5% - 2%
Organically Preserved Bases	1% - 2%
Up to 1.5%	
HP Soap 1% - 1.5%	1% - 1.5%
Up to 1%	
Bath Bombs 1%	1%
M&P Soap 0.5% - 1%	0.5% - 1%
Jelly 0.25% - 1%	0.25% - 1%
Masques 0.25% - 1%	0.25% - 1%
Shower Gel & Shampoo	0.25% - 1%
Astringent, Toner	0.25% - 1%
Bath Salt, Soak & Powder	0.25% - 1%
Household & Laundry	0.25% - 1%
Up to 0.5%	
Baby Products 0.25% - 0.5%	0.25% - 0.5%
Pet Products 0.25% - 0.5%	0.25% - 0.5%
Up to 0.1%	
Mineral Makeup (not eyes)	0.1%

About the Bulk Bases Used in this Book

There are hundreds of bulk bases at Essential Wholesale and I couldn't possibly cover them all in this book. I chose some of my favorite bulk bases to do Kitchen Chemistry projects based on versatility, costs and ingredients.

Choosing 3-1 Gels and Shampoo

All Essential Wholesale 3-1 Gels can be used as shower gel, hand soap or bubble bath. Choosing the right one for you should be based on costs, your market and what ingredients you want to use or avoid. You should also be aware of the bubble and foam potential of the product.

When you sell your products as bubble bath the FDA requires that you include the following warning statement: "Caution – Use only as directed. Extensive use or prolonged exposure may cause irritation to skin and urinary tract. Discontinue use if rash, redness or itching occurs. Consult your physician if irritation persists. Keep out of reach of children."

EW 3-1 Gel Base	Bubble Potential	Foam Potential	Sulfate Free	Cocamidopropyl Betaine Free
3-1 Basic Gel	High	High	No	No
2-1 Baby Gel	High	High	No	No
3-1 Aloe & Glycerin Gel	High	High	No	No
3-1 Aloe & Shea Gel	High	High	No	No
3-1 Coffee Gel	High	High	No	No
3-1 Herbal Wheat & Oat Gel	High	High	No	No
3-1 Amber Gel	Medium	Medium	Yes	No
2-1 Amber Baby Gel	Medium	Medium	Yes	No
3-1 Amber Citrus Gel	Medium	Medium	Yes	No
3-1 Amber Lavender Gel	Medium	Medium	Yes	No
3-1 Peppermint/TT Gel	Medium	Medium	Yes	No
3-1 Spa Herbal Gel	Medium	Medium	Yes	No
3-1 Simple Gel	Medium	Medium	Yes	No
3-1 Herbal Aloe & Shea Gel	Medium	Medium	Yes	No
3-1 Gentle Aloe Gel	Medium	Medium	Yes	No
3-1 Free & Clean Gel	Low	Low	Yes	Yes
Castile Soap	Low	Low	Yes	Yes

3-1 Clear Gel (Sulfate Free)

This is my favorite sulfate free gel. It has good slip, viscosity and foam potential. I often chose this one because it is so easy to work with.

3-1 Basic Gel

This gel is a great option because it is inexpensive and very basic. It contains just the ingredients necessary to make it work well and remain stable.

3-1 Basic Thick Gel

This gel is extra thick and super basic. It gives you the ability to add your own active ingredients which makes this a great base for heavy scenting or customizing.

Basic Concentrate Crème is a simple concentrate crème that can be used for multiple purposes. It can be added to another lotion or crème base to thicken a product. It can also be mixed with herbal tinctures, essential oils, de-ionized or distilled water, fragrance oils or aloe juice to create a variety of different lotions or crèmes. It accepts additives up to one part Basic Crème Concentrate to one part added liquids total weight.

Body Linen Spray Base is an unscented stably preserved base that can be used for body, air or linen sprays. I love this base because it is so flexible and can be used for any water based recipe.

Grapefruit Astringent

This is a great base from which to start any astringent for chaotic skin. I use it in this book to create one of our discontinued retail products that was extremely popular. If you want to start with an unscented toner base I recommend using the body linen spray base.

Colorless Liquid Foundation

The Colorless Foundation Base is designed for you to use to create your own liquid foundation colors. This base can be used to blend your own minerals, zinc, titanium dioxide and/or iron oxide to create unique shades or add Essential Wholesale powder foundation colors to create heavy or light coverage foundations. The Colorless Liquid Foundation Base offers great versatility to allow you to create stable liquid mineral foundations. The preservative system of this product is designed to allow for the addition of essential oils, fragrance oils, mica, minerals, zinc oxide, titanium dioxide and/or iron oxide ONLY anywhere from .5% all the way up to 15% overall of the approved ingredients.

Melt and Pour Lip Balm

This premade lip balm base makes it simple to make your own lip balms and lipstick without starting from scratch.

Melt and Pour Lotion Bar

This premade lip balm base makes it simple to make your own lotion bars and massage bars without starting from scratch.

Melt and Pour Shea Butter Hard Balm

This product uses a fractionated shea butter that will not cause crystallization in your products.

Melt and Pour Vegan Lip Balm

This premade lip balm base makes it simple to make your own vegan lip balms and lipstick without starting from scratch.

Simple Lotion

Simple lotion has a great silky texture. I like it because it is natural, but has a good stable viscosity no matter what the temperature is outside.

Walnut AHA Body Exfoliant

I love this stuff. It foams and exfoliates all at the same time. It is different than oil based body exfoliants and is perfect for when you don't want to have an oily mess to clean up.

Essential Oil Blends

Throughout the Kitchen Chemistry recipes you will find many essential oil blends from Essential Wholesale. I picked my favorite essential oil blends for each of the recipes, but you are welcome to use your favorite blends or single note essential oils in place of any of the essential oils or blends used in the recipes. All of the recipes will also still work if you decide to use fragrance oils in place of essential oils.

Chapter 4
Balms, Ointments and Salves

Balms, Ointments and Salves are all interchangeable names for products that are made up of oil and waxes and are free of water. They generally contain between 0.5 and 5% essential oils. By changing the essential oils and carrier oils used in a recipe you can vary the purpose of the balm you are making.

As a general rule of thumb you can use the following percentages for balms, ointments and salves of oil to wax. Your recipe can vary depending on the wax, butters, percentage of essential oil added or climate your product will be sold in. Always be sure to determine the best temperature to pour your balm, ointment or salve into the packaging you have chosen with a test pour. If you pour your product too hot you can melt and warp some plastic packaging. With lip balms the general rule is that you shouldn't pour any hotter than 115°F. The melting point of beeswax is 144 to 147 °F and that is far above the melting point of most packaging.

Basic Percentages
Lip Balm
75-79% Oils and Butters
20-24% Beeswax
1% Vitamin E

Balms, Ointments and Salves
79-85% Oils
14-20% Beeswax
1% Vitamin E

Lotion Bar
41-45% Beeswax
54-58% Oils
1% Vitamin E

Perfume Balm
17-20% Beeswax
79-82% Oils
1% Vitamin E

In all of the following recipes you can use any essential oil or essential oil blend that you would like. I chose my favorites.

Vegan Balm Recipe
5.3 ounces Extra Virgin Olive Oil
0.7 ounces Candelilla Wax
Microwave for up to 2 minutes
0.1 ounce Vitamin E
0.2 ounce Tamanu Oil
0.1 ounce Carrot Oil
0.2 ounce Gentle Skin EO Blend

Directions: Heat olive oil and candelilla wax to melt wax in the microwave or over a burner. Off heat add vitamin E, tamanu oil, carrot oil and gentle skin essential oil blend. The gentle skin essential oil blend from Essential Wholesale contains helichrysum, tea tree, lavender and chamomile Roman and German essential oils.

Muscle Ointment Recipe
12.75 ounces Olive Oil
3 ounces Beeswax Prills
Microwave for up to 3-4 minutes
16 ounces Capsicum Butter
0.4 ounces Vitamin E
1.15 ounces Deep Tissue Essential Oil blend

Directions: Heat olive oil and beeswax prills to melt the wax in the microwave or over a burner. Off heat add capsicum butter to the hot mixture and stir to melt. Next add vitamin E and deep tissue essential oil blend. The deep tissue essential oil blend from Essential Wholesale contains basil, black pepper, Roman chamomile, chamomile blue, cinnamon, citronella, eucalyptus, everlasting, ginger, grapefruit, juniper, lemongrass, peppermint, pine, ravensara, rosemary, spearmint and oregano.

Soothing Skin Ointment Recipe
11.25 ounces Organic Olive Oil
1.6 ounces Beeswax Prills
0.8 ounces Meadowfoam Oil
Microwave for up to 3 minutes
0.5 ounces Tamanu Oil
0.2 ounces Vitamin E
0.5 ounces Gentle Skin Essential Oil blend

Directions: Heat olive oil, meadowfoam oil and beeswax prills to melt the wax in the microwave or over a burner. Off heat add tamanu oil, vitamin E and gentle skin essential oil blend. The gentle skin essential oil blend from Essential Wholesale contains helichrysum, tea tree, lavender and chamomile Roman and German essential oils.

Soothing Skin Ointment Recipe from a Base
14.5 ounces M&P Hard Shea Butter Balm
0.5 to 0.75 ounces Gentle Skin Essential Oil Blend

Directions: Simply melt the hard shea butter balm base, add gentle skin essential oil blend, stir and pour into prepared containers. The gentle skin essential oil blend from Essential Wholesale contains helichrysum, tea tree, lavender and chamomile Roman and German essential oils.

Lip Balm Recipe
2.85 ounces Extra Virgin Olive Oil
1.25 ounces Meadowfoam Oil
2.85 ounces Beeswax Prills
Microwave for 3 minutes and then add
0.05 ounces Mango Butter
2.85 ounces Vitamin E
1 tablespoon Grapefruit Essential Oil

Directions: Heat olive oil, meadowfoam oil and beeswax prills to melt the wax in the microwave or over a burner. Off heat add mango butter, vitamin E and grapefruit essential oil. You can use any essential oil or blend that has a pleasant taste like lemon, lime, tangerine, mandarin, sweet orange, peppermint, spearmint, cinnamon leaf, allspice, anise, bergamot, blood orange, sweet fennel or ginger.

Lip Balm Recipe from a Base
14.5 ounces M&P Lip Balm Base
4 teaspoons Spearmint Essential Oil

Directions: Heat Essential Wholesale lip balm base for up to 3 minutes in the microwave, add spearmint essential oil, stir and pour into tubes or pots.

Color Cosmetics from Melt and Pour Bases

Lip sticks, stains and glosses (and even concealers) are simple to make by adding a variety of colorants to melt and Pour Lip bases or to your own lip balm recipe. When making color cosmetics always be certain that the ingredient you are using is approved by the FDA for the area of the face it is designed to be applied to. Here is a helpful chart to get you started.

EW DIY Color	Eyes	Lips	Face
White Shimmer	Yes	Yes	Yes
Bronze	Yes	Yes	Yes
Tangerine	Yes	Yes	Yes
Nude	Yes	Yes	Yes
Copper	Yes	Yes	Yes
Metallic Pink	Yes	Yes	Yes
Neon Pink	Yes	Yes	Yes
Gold Green	Yes	Yes	Yes
Shimmery Sage	Yes	No	Yes
Golden Yellow	Yes	Yes	Yes
Dark Silver	Yes	Yes	Yes
Purple	Yes	No	Yes
Gold Salmon	Yes	Yes	Yes
Neon Blue Green	Yes	No	Yes
Pink	Yes	Yes	Yes
Pink Purple	Yes	Yes	Yes
Gold	Yes	Yes	Yes
Mint Green	Yes	No	Yes
Bronze Green	Yes	Yes	Yes
Pearl	Yes	Yes	Yes
Blue	Yes	No	Yes
Blue Violet	Yes	No	Yes
Gold Pink	Yes	Yes	Yes
Bismuth Oxychloride C876101	Yes	Yes	Yes
Chrome Oxide Green C616735	Yes	No	Yes
Manganese Violet C43001	Yes	Yes	Yes
Black Iron Oxide C335198	Yes	Yes	Yes
Brown Iron Oxide C33115	Yes	Yes	Yes
Soft-Tex Russett Iron Oxide C337721	Yes	Yes	Yes
Ultramarine Blue Iron Oxide C431810	Yes	No	Yes
Yellow Iron Oxide C338073	Yes	Yes	Yes
D&C Orange 5 Aluminum Lake C14038	Yes	No	Yes
FD&C Blue 1 Aluminum Lake C394433	Yes	Yes	Yes
FD&C Yellow 5 Aluminum Lake C69002	Yes	Yes	Yes
D&C Red 28 Aluminum Lake C146623	No	Yes	Yes
FD&C Red 40 C37-6340	Yes	Yes	Yes

Magenta Lip Stick Recipe from a Base

5 ounces Vegan Melt & Pour Lip Balm
0.2 ounces D&C Red 27 Powder
0.5 ounces Red 180 Iron Oxide
0.05 ounces Pearl Color Powder
0.05 ounces Lip Plumping Essential Oil Blend

Directions: Heat Essential Wholesale lip balm base for up to 3 minutes in the microwave, add D&C Red 27, red 180 iron oxide, pearl (if you would like a matte finish skip the white shimmer) and lip plumping essential oil blend and stir with an immersion stick blender. Pour into tubes, pots or lipstick molds. Lip plumping essential oil blend from Essential Wholesale contains cinnamon, anise, ginger, lemon, helichrysum and basil. Due to the D&C colorant in this recipe this product will stay on the lips longer than one made with only iron oxides.

Red Lipstick Recipe from a Base
14.5 ounces Melt & Pour Lip Balm
0.9 ounces Red Iron Oxide 180
0.2 ounces Red Iron Oxide 150
0.1 ounces by weight White Shimmer
0.3 ounces Lip Plumping Essential Oil Blend

Directions: Heat Essential Wholesale lip balm base for up to 3 minutes in the microwave, add red iron oxide 180 and red iron oxide 150 and white shimmer (if you would like a matte finish skip the pearl color), and lip plumping essential oil blend and stir with an immersion stick blender. Pour into tubes, pots or lipstick molds. Lip plumping essential oil blend from Essential Wholesale contains cinnamon, anise, ginger, lemon, helichrysum and basil.

Lilac Concealer Recipe from a Base
14.5 ounces Melt and Pour Lip Balm
4.65 ounces Titanium Dioxide
0.2 ounces Manganese Violet

Caution: This product is simple to make, but the color is heat sensitive. You must pour your entire mixture all at once. If you reheat the mixture once the colors have been added you will lose the lilac color and will be left with a gray product. Once you start this project be ready to pour it all at once.

Directions: Heat Essential Wholesale lip balm base for 3-4 minutes in the microwave. Make sure it is thoroughly melted. Add titanium dioxide and mix with an immersion stick blender. This is your last chance to heat this product. If you see any signs of cooling put this whole mixture back into the microwave and warm it up. Now you are ready to add the manganese violet. Blend thoroughly with an immersion stick blender and pour immediately into your prepared containers. If for any reason you have to reheat your product you will need to re-add the manganese violet color again as a last resort.

Chapter 5
Whipped Butter

Whipped butter recipes are time consuming and labor intensive, but the resulting product is often worth every ounce of effort. The process of whipping butters while cooling quickly eliminates the problem of crystallization that often happens when shea butter is heated and cooled. It can also happen with mango and cocoa. The only other way to avoid crystals in shea butter is to use a fractionated shea butter that has filtered off the short-chain fatty acids that form crystals.

Grapefruit Whipped Butter Recipe
110 ounces Shea Butter, Naturally Refined
21 ounces Meadowfoam Oil, Refined
26 ounces Olive Oil, Virgin
0.05 ounces Carrot Oil
0.05 ounces Avocado Oil
0.05 ounces Tamanu Oil
0.05 ounces Rosehip Oil
0.05 ounces Evening Primrose Oil
0.05 ounces Vitamin E
6 ounces Pink Grapefruit Essential Oil

Directions: Add meadowfoam, olive, carrot, tamanu, rosehip and evening primrose oil together and heat oils on medium to medium high to 180°F. Remove from heat and add shea butter and melt. If the shea butter doesn't fully melt you can use low heat to finish melting it for a few minutes. Once everything is completely melted remove the product from heat and began mixing with a hand mixer. Put it in the freezer and check it often. When it starts to cloud remove it from the freezer and whip it again. Return it to the freezer for about 20-30 minutes. Once it starts to look like butter or forms an opaque layer over the top remove it from the freezer and whip it again. Repeat until the product starts to look white. When it does whip it, then add the grapefruit essential oil, whip it thoroughly again and return it to the freezer. Repeat until the product solidifies and starts to look like a solid. Whip it one last time, set it on the counter to return to room temperature. Once it is at room temperature you can package it. You will need to scoop the product into jars, tap the jar to remove air bubbles and repeat until the jar is filled.
I know this product takes a lot of babysitting but it is well worth the effort.

Grapefruit Whipped Butter Recipe on a Budget
110 ounces Shea Butter
45.65 ounces Carrier Oil of Your Choice
1.65 ounces Vitamin E
2 to 6 ounces Grapefruit Essential Oil

Directions: Follow the same process as the recipe above. This recipe has a higher percentage of Vitamin E than the one above, because the Meadowfoam, in the more expensive version, acts to keep the oils from going rancid. In this formula the Vitamin E will play that role.

Mint Chocolate Whipped Butter Recipe
0.05 ounces Tamanu Oil
0.05 ounces Carrot Oil
0.05 ounces Kukui Nut Oil
3.2 ounces Olive Oil
8.8 ounces Natural Cocoa Butter
3 ounces Shea Butter
0.25 ounces Peppermint 3rd Essential Oil
0.01 ounces Deep Tissue Essential Oil Blend

Directions: Melt the cocoa butter first and then add tamanu, carrot, kukui nut and olive oil. Off heat add shea butter. Whip this mixture together for 2-3 minutes. Set in the freezer for 10 minutes and when you see a fine layer of solids forming around the edges remove it to mix again. Return it to the freezer for another 10 minutes and whip it thoroughly. Add the peppermint essential oil and deep tissue essential oil blend whip it thoroughly again and return it to the freezer. Repeat until the product solidifies and starts to look like a solid. Whip it one last time, set it on the counter to return to room temperature. Once it is at room temperature you can package it. You will need to scoop the product into jars, tap the jar to remove air bubbles and repeat until the jar is filled.

Lime Almond Butter Recipe
16 ounces Bitter Almond Butter
½ tsp. Lime Essential Oil

Directions: Melt the bitter almond butter first and whip for 2-3 minutes. Set in the freezer for 10 to 15 minutes and when you see a fine layer of solids forming around the edges remove it to mix again. Return it to the freezer for another 10 minutes and whip it thoroughly. Add the lime essential oil, whip it thoroughly again and return it to the freezer. Repeat until the product solidifies and starts to look like a solid. Whip it one last time, set it on the counter to return to room temperature. Once it is at room temperature you can package it. You will need to scoop the product into jars, tap the jar to remove air bubbles and repeat until the jar is filled.

Options: You can follow this same process with any of the specialty butters that Essential Wholesale carries including: Broccoli Butter, Capsicum Butter, Carrot Butter, Chamomile Butter, Coffee Butter, Cranberry Butter, Ginger Butter, Jasmine Butter, Lime Butter, Mandarin Butter, Neroli Butter, Rose Butter, Rosemary Butter, Tamanu Butter, Vanilla Butter, Vitamin A Butter and/ or Vitamin E Butter.

Chapter 6
Home and Laundry Recipes

Reed diffusers are all the rage these days. They are super simple to make. These two recipes are based off of the square and round bottles carried by Essential Wholesale. You can make your batch any size to fit the containers of your choice.

Citrus Reed Diffuser Recipe
9.6 ounces Dipropylene Glycol
3.2 ounces Lime Essential Oil
0.8 ounces Litsea Essential Oil
2.4 ounces Orange 5 Fold Essential Oil

Directions: Mix all of the ingredients together, stir and pour into Square Diffuser Bottle, add reeds and use. You can store any excess product in an amber glass bottle to refill the bottle as the scent evaporates. If you are opposed to using dipropylene glycol despite its amazing safety report, you can switch it out for jojoba oil. However, be aware that if a reed diffuser full of jojoba oil spills you will have a harder time cleaning the oil out of your carpet than dipropylene glycol.

Well Being Reed Diffuser Recipe
9.6 ounces Dipropylene Glycol
6.4 ounces Well-Being Essential Oil Blend

Directions: Mix all of the ingredients together, stir and pour into Square Diffuser Bottle, add reeds and use. You can store any excess product in an amber glass bottle to refill the bottle as the scent evaporates. If you are opposed to using dipropylene glycol despite its amazing safety report you can switch it out for jojoba oil. However, be aware that if a reed diffuser full of jojoba oil spills you will have a harder time cleaning the oil out of your carpet than dipropylene glycol.

Himalayan Salt Potpourri Recipe
Scent Portion
1 ounce Dipropylene Glycol
1 ounce Peppermint 3rd Essential Oil
Potpourri Portion
Himalayan Pink Salt (Coarse)
Dried Herbs of choice (optional)

Directions: Mix dipropylene glycol with peppermint 3rd essential oils into a spray bottle and shake. This spritz should then be spritzed onto your potpourri portion and mixed. Keep the spray bottle handy to refresh your potpourri as needed. This same recipe can be used with solar salts or coarse Dead Sea salts and any herbs of your choice.

Room Mist Recipe
½ gallon Essential Wholesale Body Linen Spray Base
1 tbsp. Polysorbate 20
1 tbsp. Essential Oil of your choice

Directions: Mix polysorbate 20 and essential oil of your choice together separately. Once they are thoroughly mixed add to Essential Wholesale Body Linen Spray base or other stably preserved base and stir.

Bed Bug Spray Recipe
1/2 gallon Essential Wholesale Body Linen Spray
1 Tbsp. Neem Tincture
1 Tbsp. Lavender Essential Oil
1 Tbsp. Lavender Distillate
1 Tbsp. Polysorbate 20

Directions: Mix polysorbate 20 and lavender essential oil together in a separate container. Once they are thoroughly mixed add to Essential Wholesale Body Linen Spray base or other stably preserved base, add neem tincture and lavender distillate and mix thoroughly.

Laundry
People constantly ask me why my family smells so good. The secret is this softener brightener recipe we use in our laundry. Clothes that have been washed and dried with this smell amazing.

Softener Brightener
2.5 ounces Polysorbate 20
2 ounces Earthen EO Blend
40 ounces White Vinegar
10 ounces Hydrogen Peroxide
80 ounces Deionized or Distilled Water
Optional
2 ounces Triethanolamine (TEA)

Directions: First blend polysorbate 20 and earthen essential oil blend together thoroughly. Next add white vinegar, hydrogen peroxide and water. You can stop here or you can add TEA as a laundry booster. TEA binds to dirt and oils in your laundry and adds to the brightening properties of this recipe.

Laundry Spot Remover Recipe

8 ounces 3-1 Clear Gel (Sulfate Free)
3.2 ounces Borax
3.2 ounces Atlantic Fine Sea Salt
6.4 ounces Hydrogen Peroxide
45.6 ounces Warm Water
4 ounces White Vinegar

Directions: Add sea salt and borax to hot water, stir together to start to dissolve the solids. Then add white vinegar, hydrogen peroxide and 3-1 clear gel (no sulfate) and gently stir.

Recommendation: This is the spot remover I use for my family, but I recommend you always test any new spot remover on a small discrete spot before using it on any sentimental or expensive item.

Dish Soap Recipe

0.05 ounces Crème of Tartar
0.05 ounces Borax .05
To your dry ingredients add
0.5 ounces White Vinegar
0.25 ounces Sweet Orange Essential Oil
Stir to dissolve all the dry ingredients
16 ounces of Basic Thick 3-1 Gel

Directions: Combine crème of tartar and borax together and then add white vinegar and sweet orange essential oil to dissolve solids by stirring and then add them to 3-1 basic 3-1 gel. The added ingredients will help clean even the toughest messes.

Chapter 7
Head, Shoulders, Knees and Toes Recipes

I was wracking my brain for a title of this chapter and I didn't want to call it miscellaneous. What kept coming to mind was the line from the kid's song, "head, shoulders, knees and toes, knees and toes…" because so many body parts are covered with these products. Sometimes you just have to go with it and have fun with the way your mind works. Obviously, I did in this case.

Massage Products

Massage oils are simple to make. I'm a huge fan of using fractionated coconut oil, jojoba oil and/or meadowfoam oil for massage because none of them will go rancid, which keeps your sheets from getting a rancid aroma. Other factors of importance of course are cost and the slip of the finished product. If you use oil that won't go rancid you can skip adding Vitamin E, but if you chose any other carrier oil you should add 1% vitamin E to your recipe.

Basic Massage Oil Percentages
94-99% Carrier Oil
1% Vitamin E
1-5% Essential Oil or Essential Oil Blend

Baby Massage Oil Recipe
1 ounce Jojoba or Meadowfoam Oil
1 drop Lavender Essential Oil
1 drop Roman Chamomile Essential Oil
1 drop Blue Chamomile Essential Oil

Massage Oil Directions: Add all ingredients into a glass or PET bottle and shake.

Massage Lotion Bar Recipe
2 Tbsp. Deep Tissue Essential Oil Blend
14.5 ounces Melt & Pour Lotion Bar

Directions: Melt the M&P lotion bar and then add the deep tissue essential oil blend, stir and pour into massage bar molds. The deep tissue essential oil blend at Essential Wholesale contains basil, black pepper, Roman chamomile, chamomile blue, cinnamon, citronella, eucalyptus, everlasting, ginger, grapefruit, juniper, lemongrass, peppermint, pine, ravensara, rosemary, spearmint and oregano.

Body Products

Caiden's Earthen Body Mist Recipe
½ gallon Body Linen Spray Base
1 tbsp. Polysorbate 20
1 tbsp. Earthen Essential Oil Blend

Directions: Mix polysorbate 20 and earthen essential oil blend. Once they are thoroughly mixed add to Essential Wholesale Body Linen Spray base or other stably preserved base and stir. Earthen essential oil blend at Essential Wholesale contains ylang ylang, patchouli, cedarwood and rosewood. This is Caiden's very favorite essential oil blend.

Selah's Glitter Lotion with Lime Recipe
½ gallon Simple Lotion
1/3 cup Cosmetic Glitter
1 tbsp. Lime Essential Oil

Directions: Simply mix glitter and lime essential oil into simple lotion using an immersion stick.

Walnut AHA Body Exfoliant
3 lbs. Walnut Body Polish
0.25 ounces DMAE
0.25 ounces MSM
0.5 ounces Multi Fruit Blend Tincture
0.5 ounces Alpha Hydroxy Liquid Bundle
0.36 ounces Peppermint 3rd Essential Oil

Directions: Mix DMAE, MSM, AHA blend, multiple fruits tincture and peppermint essential oil together in a separate container. Then mix it all into walnut body polish and then stir gently with a stainless steel spoon.

Men's Body Wash Recipe
1/2 gallon 3-1 Basic Gel
2 tsp. Forest Essential Oil Blend
1/4 tsp. Green Chromium Oxide

Directions: In a separate bowl add forest essential oil blend and chrome oxide, stir together to dissolve the chrome oxide and add this to the 3-1 basic gel. Mix this together.

Hard Wax for Hair Removal
0.9 ounces Yellow Beeswax Prills
3.1 ounces Rosin

Caution: Before you get started you must know this recipe is extremely easy to make, but nearly impossible to clean out of your pots. It should be made in the same container you are going to use it in long term or the ones in which they will be sold. Once you make this recipe in a pot it can never be used for anything else.

Directions: Add beeswax to rosin and melt on medium to medium high setting. Stir continuously to avoid burning. Once everything melts remove it from heat. It is too hot to apply to the skin at this point. Continue stirring as it cools. You will see the viscosity of the product change. Once it has thickened and cooled to at least 150°F or below.

Directions for Use: Apply a thick coat of wax using a spatula at a 45 degree angle in the direction of your hair growth. Allow the wax to cool on the skin until it becomes soft and pliable. Pull up one corner of the wax, hold the skin taunt and pull off the wax in one quick motion. If you apply the wax in too think of a layer it will become brittle and break. In order to fix this you can apply a fresh layer of warm wax over the top. This will reincorporate the brittle pieces and make it easier for it all to be removed.

All Natural Zinc Deodorant Recipe
1.6 ounces Yellow Beeswax Prills
12.8 ounces Fractionated Coconut Oil
16 ounces Zinc Oxide
0.3 ounces DeoEssence Essential Oil Blend

Directions: Melt together beeswax and fractionated coconut oil. You want it to get nice and hot because once you add the zinc oxide it will cool down quickly. Add zinc oxide and mix thoroughly with an immersion stick blender. If it cools too quickly simply put it back in the microwave for a minute. Add deoessence essential oil blend, stir and pour into deodorant tubes. The zinc oxide can leave white marks on the inside of your clothing, but because we used fractionated coconut oil it won't harm your clothing or leave a rancid odor. The deoessence essential oil blend from Essential Wholesale contains bergamot, cypress, lavender 40/42, juniper, tea tree, pink grapefruit, patchouli, and lemon essential oils.

Face Products

Chaotic Facial Astringent from Base Recipe
4 lbs. Grapefruit Astringent (1/2 Gallon)
0.5 ounces DMAE
0.5 ounces MSM
1 ounce Rooibos Tincture

Directions: This recipe was one of our best sellers at von Natur. We packaged them in jars with toner pads, which was a wonderful touch. Simply add DMAE, MSM and Rooibos Tincture to ½ gallon of Essential Wholesale Grapefruit Astringent, shake or stir to dissolve dry ingredients.

Multifruit Aftershave Splash Recipe
16 ounces Multiple Fruit Acids Blend Tincture
2.2 ounces Peppermint Distillate
2 ounces Kosher Vegetable Glycerin
Optional
0.2 ounces Polysorbate 20
0.1 ounces Peppermint 3rd Essential Oil

Directions: This recipe is self-preserving from the Multiple Fruits Acids Blend Tincture from Essential Wholesale. I do not recommend any swapping of ingredients or measurements as it will have a negative impact on the overall stability of the formula. Add multiple fruit blend tincture to peppermint distillate and kosher vegetable glycerin. If you want your product to be totally natural stop here, otherwise in a separate vessel thoroughly blend the polysorbate 20 and peppermint essential oil and then add to the rest of the batch.

Soothing Toner Recipe
Blend Separately
0.4 ounces Lavender Essential Oil
0.05 ounces Chamomile, Roman Essential Oil
0.05 ounces Chamomile, blue Essential Oil
0.05 ounces Helichrysum Essential Oil
0.5 ounces Polysorbate 20
Add to
6.4 ounces Hyaluronic Acid
64 ounces Aloe Vera Juice

Instructions: Blend the essential oils and polysorbate 20 together in a separate container. The polysorbate will emulsify the essential oils into the water portion of this recipe, which will protect the skin from accidental neat (directly on the skin) application of free-floating essential oils. Then add the essential oil mixture to the hyaluronic acid and aloe vera juice. This recipe is self-preserving from the aloe vera juice and hyaluronic acid from Essential Wholesale. I do not recommend any swapping of ingredients or measurements as it will have a negative impact on the overall stability of the formula.

Color Cosmetics

Basic Base Foundation Color Recipe from Scratch
3.15 ounces Titanium Dioxide
0.25 ounces Zinc Oxide
0.2 ounces Gold Salmon
0.1 ounces Brown Iron Oxide

Directions: Add all ingredients to a food processor. Mix for a minute or so then check to see if colors are blended. If needed shift ingredients with a spoon and mix again. This very basic mixture is designed to be a blank canvas from which you can build a large array of foundation colors. You can change this color by adding brown iron oxides to make it darker, or even a touch of black iron oxide. You can red iron oxides to a pink hue, ultramarine blue for a blue hue, yellow iron oxide for a yellow hue. If you need a very light color you can add more titanium dioxide or zinc oxide to this base. If you finished product needs more glide for application you can add 1-2% sericite mica. You can use this finished product as a loose mineral foundation or add it to Essential Wholesale Colorless Foundation Base at 0.5 to 15% to create a liquid foundation.

Heavy Coverage Liquid Foundation from Base Recipe
15 ounces Colorless Liquid Foundation
2.25 ounces Tan Opal Powder Foundation
.04 ounces Foundational Essential Oil Blend

Directions: Add tan opal and foundational essential oil blend to colorless foundation base and blend thoroughly with an immersion blender. Foundational essential oil blend contains frankincense, cistus, lavender, cedarwood, and Roman and blue chamomile. You can lower the percentage of tan opal if you want to create a light coverage foundation.

Sun Dust Body Shimmer Recipe
3 ounces Sericite Mica
0.35 ounces Glitter Powder
0.6 ounces Gold Salmon
0.3 ounces Brown Iron Oxide
2 drops Lavender Essential Oil

Directions: Add sericite mica, cosmetic glitter, gold salmon and brown oxide (skip the brown oxide if you would like your shimmer to be nearly colorless) to food processor and mix. If needed shift ingredients with a spoon and mix again. If you would like to lightly scent your product add 2 drops of lavender essential oil, which is 1/10 of a percent.

Chapter 8
Bath Salts and Soaks Recipes

The easiest bath products to make are bath salts and soaks. You can buy pre-mixed bath salts or blend your own using a variety of salts on the market. Once you pick your salt or salts, it is just a matter of determining if your salts can be completely dry or should have a light coating of carrier oil. The key to making a good bath salt is using the skin safety measure of adding an equal measure of carrier oil as essential oil whenever you go over 2% essential oil in your recipe. For 2% and below, you can create an oil-free bath salt safely. For 2.1% and above, it is best to coat the salt with carrier oil.

Basic Percentages

2% and Under
16 ounces Any Salt
.32 ounces Most Any Essential Oil

2.1 to 5%
16 ounces Any Salt
0.34 Up to 0.8 ounces Most Any Essential Oil
0.34 Up to 0.8 ounces Any Carrier Oil

Himalayan Pink & Peppermint Bath Salts Recipe
37.2 ounces Solar Salt
19.5 ounces Pink Himalayan Salt
1 tsp of Fractionated Coconut Oil
1 tsp of Triple Distilled Peppermint Essential Oil (1%)

Directions: With a gloved hand or spoon mix salts together, add fractionated coconut oil and essential oil.

Making Aromatherapy Bath Soaks

Bath soaks often include salts with the addition of other ingredients to enhance the bathing experience. A warm bath can increase the rate of absorption of essential oils. In warm bath water, essential oils penetrate the skin 100 times faster than water does and 10,000 times faster than the ions of sodium and chloride from salt (Römmelt et al 1974, Schilchler 1985). Bathing also involves inhalation of essential oils as well as absorption through the skin.

You can buy ready-made soaks or create your own. To create a detoxifying aromatherapy bath, choose your favorite, unscented salt. A good salt for detoxifying is Dead Sea salt, but any salt will work. Essential oils can be added to the dry salt at 1% by adding five drops of essential oil to every one ounce of salt. If you would like to make a stronger soak you can add up to 15 drops of essential oil to every one ounce of salt, but you must also add 15 drops of a carrier oil to the salts to protect the skin while in the water. Bath soaks generally use 2% or below essential oils because the addition of a carrier oil just makes a soak look like a gloopy mess.

Luxurious Goat Milk Bath Soak Recipe
Dry Ingredients
0.5 lbs. Sodium Bicarbonate
0.4 lbs. Sea Salt
0.1 lbs. Goat Milk
1 Tbsp. MSM
Wet Ingredient
¼ tsp. Women's Balance Essential Oil Blend or your own blend

Directions: Add all dry ingredients to a food processor first, then add your essential oils. Turn on your food processor for under one minute to thoroughly blend the essential oils into your soak.

Chapter 9
Bath Bomb and Fizzy Recipes

The chemistry of bath bombs is simple. Do you remember the volcano project you (or your child) did in 4th grade? Well, bath bombs are pretty much the same chemistry concept, minus the smelly vinegar. The foundation of a bath bomb is the combination of sodium bicarbonate ($NaHCO_3$), which is a base, with citric acid ($C_5H_7O_5COOH$), which is a weak acid. Each of the ingredients is un-reactive when they are dry and separate from each other. Once they are combined and come in contact with water (H_2O), they create a vigorous reaction. This reaction, of an acid and a base, generates carbon dioxide (CO_2) which builds up and releases as bubbles.

The wonderful byproduct of this whole chemical reaction is the release of therapeutic essential oils into your bath water and the air around you. Bath bombs can also incorporate other beneficial ingredients into the formula that are soothing, moisturizing, or bubbly.

I've had a few people ask why my Kitchen Chemistry videos or other recipes I have shared never include the traditional bath bomb recipes that are all over the internet. There are a million and one bath bomb recipes out there on the market. The reason is simple: I don't like to share recipes that may fail depending on humidity in the air, how much witch hazel you spritz or don't spritz, or whatever other reason traditional bath bomb recipes fail. I prefer no-fail recipes over the ones that have a high failure rate. Bath bombs should be simple, but they are greatly impacted by the moisture in the air and hence temperamental.

At Essential Wholesale we used to have bath bomb machines that were custom built for us. These machines allowed us to make 12 bath bombs per machine at a time. We had four machines in total. The machine applied the right amount of pressure every time. Our recipe weighed out exactly the right amount of witch hazel per batch. And the sealed room, in which we manufactured the bath bombs, had a dehumidifier. And still, sometimes batches of bath bombs failed! Failed products are a huge waste of time, supplies, and money. I don't want to waste your time or supplies. And I especially don't want to waste your money.

The other reason I don't share those recipes is that they have already been done. There are dozens, if not hundreds, of websites out there sharing the traditional "One part citric acid, two parts sodium bicarbonate with a spritz of witch hazel" recipes. I'm not bashing the traditional bath bomb or anyone who teaches how to make them, I'm simply sharing that when I evaluated the economics of making bath bombs, my readers and I chose to go the no-fail route to save you time and money. My advice to everyone who makes traditional bath bombs is to invest in a dehumidifier. The investment will increase your profits in the end.

Bath bombs are a wonderful way to use aromatherapy in your bathtub. Here are a few fun and easy bath bomb recipes to get your creative juices flowing. You can choose to use the essential oils or essential oil blends I used or make up your own.

Fizzing Bath Powder Recipe
1 cup Sodium Bicarbonate
1/2 cup Citric Acid
1/4 cup Corn Starch
1 Tbsp. Pink Clay
1/4 cup Dendritic Salt
1 Tbsp. Taming the Wild Child EO Blend (from Essential Wholesale)

Directions: Mix together with gloved hands and package into air tight containers or bags. Really, it is that simple.

Messy Cupcakes Recipe
2 cups Sodium Bicarbonate
1 cup Citric Acid
2 tsp. Lavender 40/42 Essential Oil
Spritz
Witch Hazel USP

Directions: Mix ingredients together with gloved hands and pack into cupcake molds, with or without cupcake liners. If you pack each mold with an even top you will only get a slightly messy cupcake. In order to create a very messy cupcake you must create a packed, rounded top first. Once you are happy with the level of your cupcake, spritz the top heavily with witch hazel. It will start to fizz like crazy, so let it go. If you get too much overflow you can push the sides in when it is just starting to dry and is pliable.

Bubble Bars Recipe
Dry Ingredients
1 cup Sodium Bicarbonate
1 cup Crème of Tartar
2/3 cup Sodium Lauryl Sulfoacetate (SLSA)
1 tsp. Sea Kelp Powder (optional)

Wet Ingredients
1/4 cup Bio-Terge 804
3 Tbsp. Cocamidopropyl Betaine
2 tsp. Breathe Green Essential Oil Blend

Directions: First, mix all of the dry ingredients together with a gloved hand, while breaking up any clumps. Then, add all of the wet ingredients and continue mixing until it feels like a sticky dough. You can press this into a mold, or roll the dough into a log and cut it into slices while it is still soft. If you wait too long it will become very hard to cut.

Bubble bars were made popular by LUSH in the past decade, but good working recipes on how to make them have been hard to come by. I created this one that is very simple and looks just like the ones made popular by LUSH. You can add any color of your choice and essential oils to create your own varieties from this recipe.

No Fail Foaming Bath Bombs Recipe
Dry Ingredients
1 cup Citric Acid
2 cups Sodium Bicarbonate
¼ cup of Sodium Lauryl Sulfoacetate (SLSA)
¼ cup Cream of Tartar
Wet Ingredients
½ cup melted Deodorized Cocoa Butter
1 tsp. Laurel Leaf Essential Oil

Directions: Chop up the cocoa butter and melt it in the microwave or on a stove top and set aside. Chopping up the cocoa butter allows it to melt faster due to its high melting point. First, mix all of the dry ingredients with a gloved hand. Then pour in all of your wet ingredients and continue mixing. Press your mixture into a dry soap mold or cupcake tin and transfer it to the freezer for 10 to 20 minutes. Remove from the freezer and unmold. If you are patient, you can skip using the freezer and simply allow these to set up over a 12 to 24 hour period and then unmold.

Lavender Kaolin Bath Fizzies Recipe
Dry Ingredients
2 cups Sodium Bicarbonate
1 cup Citric Acid
2 Tbsp. Kaolin Clay
Wet Ingredients
1.4 ounces by weight Deodorized Cocoa Butter
1 Tbsp. Lavender Essential Oil

Directions: Chop up deodorized cocoa butter and melt it in the microwave or on a stove top and set aside. Chopping up the cocoa butter allows it to melt faster. Next, mix all of the dry ingredients with a gloved hand. Then pour in all of your wet ingredients and continue mixing. Press your mixture into a dry soap mold or cupcake tin and transfer it to the freezer for 10 to 20 minutes. Remove it from the freezer and unmold. If you are patient, you can skip using the freezer and simply allow these to set up over a 12 to 24 hour period and then unmold.

Detoxifying Bentonite Bath Fizzies Recipe
Dry Ingredients
2 cups Sodium Bicarbonate
1 cup Citric Acid
2 tablespoons Bentonite clay
Wet Ingredients
1.4 ounces Kokum Butter by weight
1 tablespoon of Cleanse Essential Oil Blend

Directions: Chop up kokum butter and melt it in the microwave or on a stove top and set aside. Chopping up the kokum butter allows it to melt faster since, like cocoa butter, it has a high melting point. Next, mix all of the dry ingredients with a gloved hand. Then pour in all of your wet ingredients and continue mixing. Press your mixture into a dry soap mold or cupcake tin, and transfer to the freezer for 10 to 20 minutes. Remove from the freezer and unmold. If you are patient, you can skip using the freezer and simply allow these to set up over a 12 to 24 hour period and then unmold.

Chocolate Butter Bath Bombs Recipe
.495 lbs. Citric Acid
.565 lbs. Sodium Bicarbonate
.25 lbs. Natural Cocoa Butter
.01 lbs. Sweet Orange Essential Oil

Directions: Chop up cocoa butter and melt it in the microwave or on a stove top and set aside. Chopping the cocoa butter up allows it to melt faster due to its high melting point. Next mix all of the dry ingredients with a gloved hand. Then, pour in all of your wet ingredients and continue mixing. Press your mixture into a dry soap mold or cupcake tin, and transfer to the freezer for 10 to 20 minutes. Remove from the freezer and unmold. If you are patient, you can skip using the freezer and simply allow these to set up over a 12 to 24 hour period and then unmold.

No-Bake Bath Cookies Recipe
Dry Ingredients
2 cups Sodium Bicarbonate
1 cup Citric Acid
1 cup Corn Starch
½ cup Epsom salts
½ cup Kaolin Clay
¼ cup Lactose
¼ cup Turbinado Sugar
Wet Ingredients
2 oz. Cocoa Butter
3 oz. Shea Butter
.5 oz. Spicy Citrus Essential Oil Blend

Directions: Chop up cocoa butter and melt it in the microwave or on a stove top and set aside, but first drop the shea butter into the melted cocoa butter to soften it up. Next, mix all of the dry ingredients with a gloved hand. Then pour in all of your wet ingredients and continue mixing. Finally, you can either hand-shape your cookies, use a cookie cutter, or use a mold to create your bath cookies. While they are soft and pliable, you can still add extra salt or sugar crystals, herbs, or anything you think will give your cookie a unique look. Let them set up for 12 to 24 hours and your cookies are all done. Just make sure you label them clearly so that no one tries to eat your bath cookies!

This No-Bake Bath Cookie recipe works much better in the tub than traditional bath cookie recipes that use egg and are baked. Baked bath cookies don't fully dissolve in the tub, but these do and they look just like real cookies.

Shower Fizzers Recipe
Dry Ingredients
2 cups Sodium Bicarbonate
1 cup Citric Acid
¼ cup Calcium Sulfate (a.k.a. Plaster of Paris)
Wet Ingredient
2 tsp. Well-Being Essential Oil Blend
Spritz
Witch Hazel USP

Directions: Mix ingredients together with gloved hands and pack into soap molds and allow to harden over one to two hours.

Baked Bath Cookies
Baked Bath Cookies are beautiful to look at and offer an amazing aroma, but they are a bit odd when you toss them in your bath water. Just imagine

dropping a real cookie in your bath water. On the good side, they sure look cute and they actually make your skin feel great. On the negative side they are messy in the tub and take a long time to dissolve. And maybe saying that they dissolve is giving them too much credit. They turn to mush, but they are a fun project (my girls loved helping me) and they even could be used short term as room fresheners, decor and baths.

Baked Bath Cookie Recipe
2 cups Fine Sea Salt
1/2 cup Sodium Bicarbonate
1/2 cup Cornstarch
2 T Fractionated Coconut Oil
2 Eggs
1/4 tsp Essential Oil of your choice

Directions: Preheat your oven to 350 F. Combine all the ingredients and mix thoroughly. You can form the cookies in your hand or use a cookie cutter. Gently place your "cookie" on an ungreased no stick cookie sheet. You can sprinkle them then with herbs, large sugar or salt.
Bake the "cookies" for ten minutes, until they are lightly browned. Allow the bath cookies to cool completely.

To use: Drop 1 "cookie" into a warm bath and allow to dissolve. Yield: 24 cookies or less depending on the size of your "cookies."

Chapter 10
A Word about Soap and Recipes

I am not providing recipes for cold process, hot process and melt and pour soap in this book because I believe that it is important to read a thorough book on how to make each of the forms of soap from scratch, rather than to use a recipe out of context of the process. There are many wonderful books and tutorials on cold and hot process. To learn how to make your own melt and pour soap see my book, How to Make Melt and Pour Soap Base from Scratch, for methodology, recipes and troubleshooting information.

About Cold Processed Soap and Essential Oils

In the process of manufacturing cold process soap, essential oils are added before the lye has been consumed, which means it is highly alkaline. Cold process soapmakers try to work around potential problems by choosing essential oils that are resistant to strong alkali or can accommodate the changes that occur in non-resistant scents and colors.

According to Kevin Dunn, in an interview with Robert Tisserand,
"Essential oils are complex mixtures of dozens of chemical compounds. A given essential oil may contain some compounds that react with alkali, and others that do not. Lavender oil, for example, contains about 42% linalool (which does not react) and 22% linalyl acetate (which does). In fact, when linalyl acetate reacts with alkali, one of the products is linalool. Thus the scent of a CP soap made with lavender oil will smell less of linalyl acetate and more of linalool than the original essential oil.

The only way to predict which essential oils will react with alkali is to examine the list of components and note which of them are reactive. Such compounds generally consist of esters, phenols, and acids. There is a practical way, however, for a soapmaker to evaluate essential oil reactivity. Add a few drops of essential oil to 1 mL of the lye solution used for soapmaking (typically 25-50% NaOH). A reaction will be visible and sometimes not. In either case, wait a day or two and then compare the scent of the alkaline EO to that of the original. In some cases, there will be no difference in scent. In those cases where the scent changes, the alkaline scent might not be bad, just different from the original.

Phenols and acids react directly with alkali to produce odorless salts. Clove oil for example, contains a large proportion of eugenol (a phenol). If you add a few drops of clove oil to lye as described above, the resulting solution is bright yellow and very nearly odorless. Esters, on the other hand, are decomposed by lye into an acid salt (usually odorless) and an alcohol, which is often fragrant. In fact, the alcohol produced is often present as one of the components of the original EO. The scent of such an EO changes as the proportions of its components change, but it remains fragrant.

Phenols are harder to spot, but the most common fragrant phenols are eugenol (clove, cinnamon leaf), carvacrol (thyme, oregano), thymol (thyme), and vanillin (vanilla). Phenols are actually weak acids. Other fragrant acids typically smell sour, e.g. acetic acid in vinegar."
Kevin Dunn, Caveman Chemistry

About Hot Processed Soap and Essential Oils

Essential Oils do not suffer the impact of the strong alkali that cold process soap is exposed to because the scent is added as a final phase once the alkali has been consumed. Essential oils can even be added to hot process liquid soap when it is completely done processing and has cooled, because the soap is in liquid form. You should be aware that when essential oils are added to completed hot process liquid soap when it has cooled, some of those essential oils will separate. You will need to give a "shake before use" direction on your label.

Recipes Using Hot Processed Soap
This Yoga mat spray uses castile soap, which is hot process soap. It is a bit different than many of the yoga mat sprays available on the market today. Typical yoga mat sprays contain alcohol, or witch hazel (which contains alcohol), or vinegar, or are simply a mixture of essential oils with water. In my opinion, alcohol is drying to surfaces, vinegar is good for cleaning non porous materials, and essential oils in water are an air freshener and not a cleanser. This recipe is simple, clean and effective.

Yoga Mat Cleansing Spray Recipe
½ tsp Tea Tree Essential oil .05 ounces by weight
½ tsp Patchouli essential oil .05 ounces by weight
½ tsp Lemongrass essential oil .05 ounces by weight
2 tablespoons Lavender essential oil .7 ounces by weight
3 Tablespoons Polysorbate 20 which is 1.5 ounces by weight
1 cup Deionized or Distilled Water 8 ounces by weight
2 cups Liquid Castile Soap 17.2 ounces by weight

Directions: Add tea tree, patchouli, lemongrass, lavender and polysorbate 20 and mix thoroughly. Add essential mixture to water and stir. Then add this mixture to the castile soap. This cleanser can be used for daily cleansing or deep cleaning of your yoga mat.

No Bump, No Razor Burn Shaving Soap Crème Recipe
2 tsp. of Tartaric Acid
3 tsp. of Malic Acid
3 tsp. of Glycolic Acid
¼ of a cup of Kosher Vegetable Glycerin
1/3 cup of Certified Organic Multifruit Tincture
2 cups Castile Soap
½ of a gallon Essential Wholesale Basic Concentrate Crème
15 drops Tea Tree Essential Oil
30 drops Lavender Essential Oil
3 Tablespoons Peppermint 3rd Distilled

Directions: Add tartaric, malic, glycolic acids, kosher vegetable glycerin, multifruit tincture and liquid castile soap together and stir to dissolve. Next, add Essential Wholesale Basic Concentrate Crème, tea tree, lavender and peppermint essential oil. Now you are ready to mix with an immersion blender.

About Melt and Pour Soap

When using essential oils with low boiling points, it is important to add your essential oils to your melt and pour soap at the lowest possible temperature. Melt and pour soap is still pourable at 130 degrees Fahrenheit, which allows you to choose the optimal temperature to add your essential oils before pouring, based on the boiling point of the essential oil used.

Melt and pour soap is the simplest soap making technique, even if you make it from scratch and don't use an already prepared base. In this section I will cover the basics that can get you started with melt and pour soap.

Melting Soap
The soap base must be heated in a suitable vessel. I recommend stainless steel for stove top or Pyrex for microwaving. Chop up your soap base into smaller chunks. This will make melting faster and with a more even temperature. You can melt it in the microwave for 30 seconds up to 1 minute at a time. When microwaving, cover with saran wrap to help trap moisture and reduce evaporation.

Heating should be done carefully to avoid over-heating it. If you overheat the soap, it can become discolored and the texture may be adversely affected. However, now that you know the inside scoop on Melt and Pour Soap Base recipes, you might know a trick or two to fix it. The addition of Propylene Glycol can make up for overheating and the loss of moisture by evaporation. Also, a discolored yellow hue may be caused by excessive evaporation and can be fixed with the addition of Propylene Glycol. The addition of TEA will help if clouding occurs.

Soap Molds
Use soap molds that are made of a suitable material that is able to handle soap temperatures between 135 °F and 155 °F. You can use flexible silicone molds, heavy duty molds, industrial molds and single cavity and trays molds.

Coloring Your Soap
The easiest method for coloring your soap is to use cosmetic grade, water based liquid colors. You can also use iron oxides, ultramarines, micas and natural ingredients with stable colors. Examples of cosmetic grade colorants are ones that have FD&C (Food, Drug and Cosmetic) or D&C (Drug and Cosmetic) in the name. If you use cosmetic grade colorants remember, just a tiny bit of color goes a long way. Make sure you thoroughly stir FD&C and D&C colors into your hot melted soap base prior to pouring it into molds.

All iron oxides and ultramarines can be easily identified by their names and they are available in powder form. The easiest way to add iron oxides and ultramarines to your Melt and Pour Soap base is to saturate and mix them with a little denatured alcohol. Then add this blend into your melted soap base.

Micas come in a large variety of colors. They add glimmer, shimmer and fun to your soap. Micas often have other additives so be sure to read the ingredient list and fully disclose them on your finished product.

Natural Ingredients provide some fabulous hues and give your soap a beautiful appearance along with bonus side benefits. A few great examples include beta carotene, blue green algae and kelp, as well as green, pink, rhassoul and bentonite clay. Use a stick blender when adding heavy powders to fully incorporate them into your base before pouring. The best way to do this without creating too many bubbles is to use your blender to mix the clay into a slurry by taking ¼ of the soap you plan on using and then stir the slurry into the remaining soap. If you use clay you should add a preservative. Clay is dirt after all and when you add water your soap would become the perfect breeding grow for microorganisms.

A simple recipe for adding clay is:
16 ounces Melt and Pour Soap base
0.16 ounces Preservative Blend (from Essential Wholesale) or another paraben based blend
0.16 ounces Clay of your choice

Directions: Mix Preservative Blend and clay together thoroughly and stir into melted soap.

Note: Only paraben based preservatives work as a broad spectrum preservative with clay when it is hydrated. It is always good to do a test batch to see how stable your color will be. Some colors fade with exposure to light, others may react chemically with compounds in essential or fragrance oils. To test color stability, store one bar in a dark refrigerator, one bar in a room away from direct sunlight and one bar near a north facing window. It is good to find out early how your colors will stand up to the conditions they may face while in a store or with the consumer.

Scenting Your Soap

Adding essential oil or fragrance oil to your soap is super simple. The topic of whether to use essential oils or fragrance oils is a bit more complicated and I recommend reading my book *The Art, Science and Business of Aromatherapy* for more in depth information.

In general, you can scent your Melt and Pour soap between 1-3%. Certain essential oils and fragrance oils may discolor your soap immediately or over time. For instance, vanilla fragrance oil and lemongrass essential oil are well known for causing browning in your soap.
To add scent weigh the Melt and Pour Soap you will use. Multiply weight of Melt and Pour Soap base by 0.1 (for 1%), 0.2 (for 2%) or 0.3 (for 3%) and then add that to your melted soap and stir thoroughly. If you chose fragrance oils make sure that you buy cosmetic grade and not candle fragrances.

Adding Exfoliants

Adding exfoliants and herbs can create a unique and natural appearance for your finished soap base. Popular exfoliants for soap include oatmeal, coffee, poppy seeds, whole herbs, loofahs, jojoba beads, pumice and walnut powder. In order to best suspend your ingredients in your soap it is best to incorporate them by blending them into your soap base at the set up point temperature (125 °F) of your Melt and Pour Soap Base.

Embedding in M&P Soap

You can embed layers, cubes or cute molded soaps inside of other soaps. You can also embed toys and other fun objects. The trick to embedding is using low temperatures. I have had the most success pouring at 125 °F. Early in our business we owned a company called Critter Soaps that sold embedded toys in soap. The toy can be fully emerged in the soap or can be sticking out. One of our best sellers was soap with a rubber ducky that was half embedded and half way out of the soap. We packaged each of our bars clamshell packaging style. It was perfect because we poured and sold our soap in the exact same container.

For embedding toys get started by melting some soap, add fragrance and any color you desire. Fill your mold half way with soap, spritz your toy down with alcohol and then place it into the center of your soap mold. Use a spoon to fix the position of your toy if necessary and fill the rest of your mold up with soap, again using a spoon to reposition your toy if necessary. Spritz with alcohol to removed bubbles and allow it to cool.

Embedding soap into soap is a two part process. First create your color blocks of soap. You can use non-bleeding colorants and create a huge variety of options. You can use cute soap or candy molds or simple molds and cut colorful pieces into cubes and strips. Once you have colorful soaps to embed you can get started on step two. Melt uncolored or white soap, scent it as desired and then pour it into your soap loaf or mold. Fill your mold about one third full, when your soap is 125 °F spritz your colored embedding pieces with alcohol and drop them in, repeat until your loaf is full.

Swirling M&P Soap
Swirling M&P soap is relatively easy, but time consuming. To get started melt 2 lbs. of crystal clear M&P soap and scent it as desired. Pour one layer of soap into your mold and allow it to fully harden and then spritz with alcohol. In a separate container pour about 4 to 6 ounces of your scented M&P soap and add a colorant, mix thoroughly and then pour this over your first layer and spritz with alcohol. Your next layer should be a contrasting color. Once you have it prepared pour it in an "S" pattern over your 2nd layer, run a spoon or fork through the center of the "S" and spritz. Once that one develops a thin skin you can pour your next layer. Repeat the entire process over and over again until you have filled your mold with layers of soap. This time consuming process does produce a very cool looking soap and is easiest when you keep your soap at a low temperature for pouring and use non-bleeding colors. I am fond of using micas and natural ingredients for that very reason.

Layer M&P Soap
In separate containers melt the soap for all of the layers of your project. This will allow all of the layers to be at the same temperature as you work on this recipe. If you are making three layered soap you would have three containers of soap ready at the same time. Scent all three containers of soap with the same essential oils, but color each with contrasting colors. Pour your first layer, spritz it with alcohol and allow it to cool and form a solid film over the top. The first layer will cool faster than your other prepared containers of soap because of the surface area. Make sure your second layer of soap is still pourable and not too hot before pouring it over your first layer. If your prepared layers have cooled too much, pop it in the microwave. Just be certain it isn't hotter than 125 °F when you pour.

Pouring Your Soap into Molds

Depending on your soap mold, it is best to pour your finished soap between 135 °F and 155 °F. Pour your soap slowly and evenly into sanitized soap molds. Spray surface of soap with denatured alcohol to eliminate bubbles created while pouring warm soap into molds.

Unmolding Your Soap

In the ideal world you would allow your soap to completely cool for 12 to 24 hours and simply slip it out of the mold. But in   today's fast paced world we all want our soap, and we want it now! If you can wait, simply allow your soap to cool completely for 12 to 24 hours and then apply pressure to the back of the mold and your soap should pop right out. If you don't want to wait you can use the freezer method. As soon as your soaps have set-up slightly, place the molds gently into the freezer. This is the easiest and quickest method to get the soap to release from a mold. You can leave the soap in freezer for approximately 10-20 minutes. Don't leave the soap in the freezer too long. Remove the mold from the freezer and allow the soap to sit for about 5 minutes. The soap will be easy to remove. Simply turn the mold over and apply pressure to the back. Be prepared to catch it or gently release the soap onto a hard surface.

Packaging Your Soap

When the soap bar has been removed from the mold and is at room temperature it should be wrapped to retain an attractive appearance. You can use shrink wrap, clear plastic food wrap used with a heat gun, cellophane bags, or other attractive plastic bags. Your soap should be stored at room temperature.

Labeling Your Soap

Remember your soap is a cosmetic and by law must be labeled appropriately. Use the ingredient lists I have provided with each recipe and don't forget to include any additives you add to your finished product. You must use INCI names for anything you add to your soap. For your convenience you can find complete list of INCI names on the Essential Wholesale website.

Felted Soap

Melt and Pour Soap or Cold Processed Soap
Fiber Roving

Directions: Felted Soap is a bit time consuming, but it sure does make a cool finished product. You start out with one bar of either cold processed soap or melt and pour soap and fiber roving. Simply wrap your bar of soap with a length of roving and dampen it with hot water. Now the long process, felt is tangled wool so your job is to agitate the wool by flipping the soap bar round and round in your hands in every direction. As the wool tangles you are ready to add a length of roving in the opposite direction, dampen your soap again and start agitating the wool fibers. This entire process can take up to five minutes. You can squeeze out the excess water by wrapping it into a piece of bubble wrap and squeezing. Allow your bar to dry for 24 hours. Felted soap is a great way to save an ugly bar of soap and creates a permanent wash cloth around your bar of soap.

Jelly Roll Soap Loaves
White Layer
7 ounces White Melt & Pour Soap
2 ounces Vegetable Glycerin
1 tsp Taming the Wild Child Essential Oil Blend
Colored Layer
7 ounces Crystal Clear Melt & Pour Soap
2 ounces Vegetable Glycerin
1 teaspoon Taming the Wild Child Essential Oil Blend
1 teaspoon Gold DIY Mineral Makeup

Directions: Melt in separate containers both the white melt and pour soap and the crystal clear melt and pour soap. This will allow both layers to be at the same temperature as you work on this recipe. To the white melt and pour soap add glycerin and taming the wild child essential oil blend and stir. Pour this into a square flexible mold and spritz the top with alcohol. Get to work right away on your second layer by adding glycerin and taming the wild child essential oil blend to your crystal clear melt and pour soap along with the gold DIY mineral makeup. Stir thoroughly. When the white layer has a layer of cooled soap on top and the gold layer is 130 °F you are ready to pour the colored layer evenly across the top. Your soap will be ready to roll within a few minutes. Wait for it to pliable but not squishy. I like to pull mine out of the mold at 104 °F. After you remove it from the mold apply firm and even pressure as you slowly roll your soap. Continue rolling and evening out the shape of your roll as you work with it.

Dead Sea Salt & Sea Kelp Soap Loaf
¾ cup Course Dead Sea Salt
2 Tbsp. Ripple Reducer Essential Oil Blend
1 Tbsp. Atlantic Kelp
3 lbs. of White M&P Soap

Directions: Pour a thin layer of course Dead Sea salt along the bottom of your soap loaf pan. Melt your melt and pour soap. You can use any brand, use a kit from Essential Wholesale or make your soap from scratch. Add Atlantic sea kelp and ripple reducer essential oil blend and stir, if necessary use an emersion blender to mix it in thoroughly. You can use any essential oil or essential oil blend that you prefer. The ripple reducer essential oil blend at Essential Wholesale contains juniper, lavender, geranium, bergamot, chamomile, rosemary, grapefruit and fennel. Next prepare the salts by pouring a shallow layer of soap over the salts in the mold, stir to insure that all of the salts are coated with soap and then proceed to pour the rest of the soap into the mold. Allow it to cool thoroughly before unmolding.

Solid Shea Butter Sugar Scrub Recipe
6 ounces Melt and Pour Soap Base
4 ounces Shea Butter
11.5 ounces Turbinado Raw Sugar
0.2 ounces Peppermint Essential Oil Blend

Directions: Heat up your Melt and Pour Soap Base (you can use any brand on the market or any of the soap base recipes from my book How to Make Melt and Pour Soap Base from Scratch.) Add shea butter and allow it to melt into the hot soap and next, stir in peppermint essential oil. Your product will be poured into soap molds, so once you are ready to pour add turbinado raw sugar to your melted soap, stir and pour quickly into soap molds. Allow your product to cool for 2-4 hours before un-molding.

Apendix 1
Weights and Measurements

WEIGHTS and MEASUREMENTS GUIDE

When you are measuring your ingredient choose to measure by either weight or by volume. As much as possible, do not switch back and forth. Eventually, you will have to make larger batches and will need to convert your formulas. It is best if you start all of your formulas measuring by weight. When you are ready to make larger batches you will not want to have to measure out your ingredients by the cup. Every ingredient has a different specific gravity, meaning 1 cup of feathers does not weigh the same as 1 cup of water. In the long run it is easier and more accurate to use weight for all of your measurements.

BY WEIGHT EQUIVALENTS			
1 ounce	.0625 lb	28.3495231 gram	.0283495 kilograms
1 lbs	16 ounces	453.59237 gram	.453592 kilograms
1 kilogram	2.2046 lbs	35.2739619 ounce	1000 grams
1 gram	.035274 ounces	.564384 lbs	0.001 kilogram
1 gallon (H_2O)	8.3453 lbs (H_2O)	133.5248 ounces*	

*Specific Gravity Varies

BY VOLUME EQUIVALENTS						
.17 fl ounce	1 teaspoon	60 drops	5 milliliters			
.5 fl ounce	1 tablespoon	180 drops	15 milliliters			
1 fl ounce	480 drops	6 teaspoons	2 tablespoons	29.57 milliliters		
8 fl ounce	3840 drops	48 teaspoons	16 tablespoons	1 cup	236.56 milliliters	
16 fl ounces	7680 drops	96 teaspoons	32 tablespoons	2 cups	1 pint	473.12 milliliters
64 fl ounce	½ gallon	30,720 drops	1892.48 milliliters			
128 fl ounce	1 gallon	64,440 drops	3784.96 milliliters			

COMMON PERCENTAGES BY WEIGHT AND VOLUME

This is a tool to determine how much of an ingredient to add based on percentages. We have left all measurements for you to decide if you would like to round up or round down. We are aware of the fact that you cannot put in 2.4 drops, but we left it up to you to decide if you want to round down to two or round up to three drops. Also, the specific gravity of every ingredient is different. We have given you the specific gravity of water. If you need to determine a different percentage than we have given, you simply multiply the percentage you want to use by the amount of product you are adding it to. For instance, to add .8 % essential oil to 1 lb of product by weight the equation would be: 1 lb x .8 % = .008 lbs. If you needed to determine how many ounces .008 lbs equaled, you would multiply .008 lbs by 16 ounces: .008 x 16 = .128 ounces.

BY WEIGHT

.5% of 1 ounce	.005 ounce	2.4 drops		
.5% of 1 lbs	.08 ounces	.005 lbs	38.4 drops	
.5% of 1 kilogram	.005 kilograms	.011 lbs	.175 ounce	5 grams
.5% of 1 gram	.000177 ounce	.0002822 lbs	.000005 kilograms	
.5% of 1 gallon (H$_2$O)	.041727 lbs (H$_2$O)	.667624 ounces*		
1% of 1 ounce	ounce	4.8 drops		
1% of 1 lbs	ounces	.01 lbs	76.8 drops	
1% of 1 kilogram	kilograms	.022 lbs	.35 ounce	10 grams
1% of 1 gram	ounce	.005644 lbs	.00001 kilograms	
1% of 1 gallon (H$_2$O)	lbs (H$_2$O)	1.335248 ounces*		
1.5% of 1 ounce	ounce	7.2 drops		
1.5% of 1 lbs	ounces	.015 lbs	115.2 drops	
1.5% of 1 kilogram	kilograms	.033 lbs	.525 ounce	15 grams
1.5% of 1 gram	ounce	.0059262 lbs	.000015 kilograms	
1.5% of 1 gallon (H$_2$O)	lbs (H$_2$O)	2.002872 ounces*		
2% of 1 ounce	ounce	9.6 drops		
2% of 1 lbs	ounces	.02 lbs	153.6 drops	
2% of 1 kilogram	kilograms	.044 lbs	.7 ounce	20 grams
2% of 1 gram	ounce	.011288 lbs	.00002 kilograms	
2% of 1 gallon (H$_2$O)	lbs (H$_2$O)	2.670496 ounces*		
2.5% of 1 ounce	ounce	12 drops		
2.5% of 1 lbs	ounces	.025 lbs	192 drops	
2.5% of 1 kilogram	kilograms	.055 lbs	.875 ounce	25 grams
2.5% of 1 gram	ounce	.01411 lbs	.000025 kilograms	
2.5% of 1 gallon (H$_2$O)	lbs (H$_2$O)	3.33812 ounces*		
3% of 1 ounce	ounce	14.4 drops		
3% of 1 lbs	ounces	.03 lbs	153.6 drops	
3% of 1 kilogram	kilograms	.066 lbs	1.05 ounce	30 grams
3% of 1 gram	ounce	.016932 lbs	.00003 kilograms	
3% of 1 gallon (H$_2$O)	lbs (H$_2$O)	4.005744 ounces*		

*Specific Gravity Varies

BY VOLUME

.5% of 1 teaspoon	.00085 fl ounces	.3 drops	.025 milliliters
.5% of 1 tablespoon	.0025 fl ounces	.9 drops	.075 milliliters
.5% of 1 fl. ounce	2.4 drops	.14785 milliliters	
.5% of 8 fl. ounces	.04 fl ounces	19.2 drops	1.1828 milliliters
.5% of 16 fl. ounces	.08 fl ounces	38.4 drops	2.3656 milliliters
.5% of 64 fl. ounces or ½ gallon	.32 fl ounces	153.6 drops	9.4624 milliliters
.5% of 128 fl. ounces or 1 gallon	.64 fl ounces	322.2 drops	18.9248 milliliters
1% of 1 teaspoon	.0017 fl ounces	.6 drops	.05 milliliters
1% of 1 tablespoon	.005 fl ounces	1.8 drops	.15 milliliters
1% of 1 fl. ounce	4.8 drops	.2957 milliliters	
1% of 8 fl. ounces	.08 fl ounces	38.40 drops	2.3656 milliliters
1% of 16 fl. ounces	.16 fl ounces	76.8 drops	4.7312 milliliters
1% of 64 fl. ounces or ½ gallon	.64 fl ounces	307.2 drops	18.9248 milliliters
1% of 128 fl. ounces or 1 gallon	1.28 fl ounces	644.4 drops	37.8496 milliliters
1.5% of 1 teaspoon	.00255 fl ounces	.9 drops	.075 milliliters
1.5% of 1 tablespoon	.0075 fl ounces	1.35 drops	.225 milliliters
1.5% of 1 fl. ounce	7.2 drops	.44355 milliliters	
1.5% of 8 fl. ounces	.12 fl ounces	57.6 drops	3.5484 milliliters
1.5% of 16 fl. ounces	.24 fl ounces	115.2 drops	7.0968 milliliters
1.5% of 64 fl. ounces or ½ gallon	.96 fl ounces	4608 drops	28.3872 milliliters
1.5% of 128 fl. ounces or 1 gallon	1.92 fl ounces	966.6 drops	56.7744 milliliters

116

BY VOLUME			
2% of 1 teaspoon	.0034 fl ounces	1.2 drops	.1 milliliters
2% of 1 tablespoon	.01 fl ounces	3.6 drops	.3 milliliters
2% of 1 fl. ounce	9.6 drops	.5914 milliliters	
2% of 8 fl. ounces	.16 fl ounces	76.8 drops	4.7312 milliliters
2% of 16 fl. ounces	.32 fl ounces	153.6 drops	9.4624 milliliters
2% of 64 fl. ounces or ½ gallon	1.28 fl ounces	614.4 drops	37.8496 milliliters
2% of 128 fl. ounces or 1 gallon	2.56 fl ounces	1288.8 drops	75.6992 milliliters
2.5% of 1 teaspoon	.00425 fl ounces	1.5 drops	.125 milliliters
2.5% of 1 tablespoon	.00125 fl ounces	4.5 drops	.375 milliliters
2.5% of 1 fl. ounce	12 drops	.73925 milliliters	
2.5% of 8 fl. ounces	.2 fl ounces	96 drops	5.914 milliliters
2.5% of 16 fl. ounces	.4 fl ounces	192 drops	11.828 milliliters
2.5% of 64 fl. ounces or ½ gallon	1.6 fl ounces	768 drops	47.312 milliliters
2.5% of 128 fl. ounces or 1 gallon	3.2 fl ounces	1661 drops	94.624 milliliters
3% of 1 teaspoon	.0051 fl ounces	1.8 drops	.15 milliliters
3% of 1 tablespoon	.015 fl ounces	5.4 drops	.45 milliliters
3% of 1 fl. ounce	14.4 drops	.8871 milliliters	
3% of 8 fl. ounces	.24 fl ounces	115.2 drops	7.0968 milliliters
3% of 16 fl. ounces	.48 fl ounces	230.4 drops	14.19636 milliliters
3% of 64 fl. ounces or ½ gallon	1.92 fl ounces	921.6 drops	56.7744 milliliters
3% of 128 fl. ounces or 1 gallon	3.84 fl ounces	1933.2 drops	113.5488 milliliters

Appendix 2
Supplies and Equipment

Business Support

Essential U Blog
www.essentialublog.com

Indie Beauty Network
www.indiebeauty.com
E-Mail: indiebusiness@gmail.com
Send an email to request the mailing
Address
Telephone: 704-291-7280

Natural Association of Holistic Aromatherapy
www.naha.org
P.O. Box 1868
Banner Elk, NC 28604
E-Mail: info@naha.org
Telephone: 828-898-6161
Fax: 828-898-1965

Contract Manufacturing

Essential Labs
www.essentiallabs.com
E-Mail: info@essentiallabs.com
Telephone: 503.905.3273

Diffusers

Amazon
www.amazon.com
Large selection of aromatherapy
diffusers

Essential Wholesale
www.essentialwholesale.com
Reed Diffuser DIY Supplies

8850 SE Herbert Court
Clackamas, Oregon 97015
Telephone: 503-722-7557

Do It Yourself Education

Kitchen Chemistry
*www.youtube.com/user/
essentialwholesale/videos*

Essential U Blog
*www.essentialublog.com/blog/
category/diy*

Make Your Cosmetics
www.makeyourcosmetics.com

Essential Oils and Ingredients

Essential Wholesale
www.essentialwholesale.com
Reed Diffuser DIY Supplies
8850 SE Herbert Court
Clackamas, Oregon 97015
Telephone: 503-722-7557

Insurance

Indie Beauty Network
www.indiebeauty.com
E-Mail: indiebusiness@gmail.com
Send an email to request the mailing
Address
Telephone: 704-291-7280

Manufacturing Equipment

Indco Mixers
www.indco.com

Jiffy Mixer Co, Inc
www.jiffymixer.com

Packaging

You can find a complete list of
Packaging Suppliers here:
www.essentialwholesale.com/
Packaging-Resources

Packaging Diva
www.packagingdiva.com

Private Label Manufacturing

Essential Labs
www.essentiallabs.com
E-Mail: info@essentiallabs.com
Telephone: 503.905.3273

Soapmaking Supplies

Certified Lye
www.certified-lye.com

Clamshell Packaging
www.clamshell-packaging.com

Essential Wholesale
www.essentialwholesale.com
Reed Diffuser DIY Supplies
8850 SE Herbert Court
Clackamas, Oregon 97015
Telephone: 503-722-7557

Soap Equipment
www.soapequipment.com

Soap Molds.com
www.soapmolds.com
2138 Humboldt St
Bellingham, WA 98226
Telephone: 360-671-0201

Appendix 3
Tradeshows and Conferences

Alliance of International Aromatherapists Conference
http://www.alliance-aromatherapists.org/

Beauty Expo
http://www.beautyexpousa.com/

Cosmoprof
http://www.cosmoprofnorthamerica.com/

HBA Global Expo
http://www.hbaexpo.com/

Global Spa Summit
http://www.globalspasummit.org/

Handcrafted Soapmakers Guild Annual Conference
http://www.soapguild.org/

Health and Nutrition Show
http://www.healthyharvestshow.com/

In-Cosmetics
http://www.in-cosmetics.com/

Indie Cruise
http://www.indiebusinessblog.com/category/cruise/

Integrative Healthcare Symposium
http://www.ihsymposium.com/12/public/enter.aspx

International Beauty Show
http://www.ibsnewyork.com/

International Congress of Esthetics and Spa
http://www.lneonline.com/tradeshows/

International Esthetics, Cosmetics & Spa Conferences
http://www.iecsc.com/

ISPA Conference & Expo
http://www.experienceispa.com/events/

Natural Products Expo
http://www.expowest.com/ew12/public/enter.aspx

Natural Beauty Summit
http://www.naturalbeautysummit.com/

Natural & Organic Products Europe
http://www.naturalproducts.co.uk/

New York International Gift Fair EX-TRACTS
http://www.nyigf.com/Home.aspx

Sustainable Cosmetics Summit
http://www.sustainablecosmeticssummit.com/

The World of Aromatherapy
http://www.naha.org/conference.htm

References

Every effort has been made to credit resources, however, 13 years of knowledge from reading books, industry magazines, websites, training material, material safety data sheets, certificate of analysis, industry sales material, personal communications and taking continuing education course has contributed to the writing of this book. If any unwitting omissions have occurred the author apologizes in advance.

California Department of Public Health,
NDMA and Other Nitrosamines - Drinking Water Issues,
http://www.cdph.ca.gov/certlic/drinkingwater/Pages/NDMA.aspx

Cosmetic Ingredient Review,
CIR Annual Report, CIR Compendium, CIR Ingredient Reports,
http://www.cir-safety.org/publications.shtml

Cosmetic Ingredient Review,
Quick Reference Table, Cosmetics Ingredient Reports through June 2010,
http://www.cir-safety.org/staff_files/PublicationsListDec2009.pdf

Cosmetic Ingredient Review,
Quick Reference Table, Cosmetics Ingredient Reports through June 2010,
http://www.cir-safety.org/staff_files/PublicationsListDec2009.pdf

Cosmetics and Toiletries,
Cosmetics Registration in California and the FDA's Electronic-only Drug Registration, David Steinberg, Vol.124, No.10/October 2009

Epsom Salt Council,
About Epsom Salt, The Science of Epsom Salt,
http://www.epsomsaltcouncil.org/about/

Essential U blog,
various,
http://www.essentialublog.com

Essential Wholesale,
MSDS and Certificate of Analysis Databases

European Commission, Health and Consumers, Cosmetics-CosIng,
http://ec.europa.eu/consumers/cosmetics/cosing/

European Commission, Health and Consumers, Cosmetics-CosIng,
Annexes,
http://ec.europa.eu/consumers/cosmetics/cosing/index.cfm?fuseaction=ref_data.annexes_v2

European Commission, Health and Consumers, Cosmetics-CosIng,
Regulations and Directives,
http://ec.europa.eu/consumers/cosmetics/cosing/index.cfm?fuseaction=ref_data.regulations

FDA, U.S. Food and Drug Administration,
Cosmetics,
http://www.fda.gov/Cosmetics/default.htm

FDA, U.S. Food and Drug Administration,
Cosmetics Labeling and Label Claims,
http://www.fda.gov/Cosmetics/CosmeticLabelingLabelClaims/default.htm

FDA, U.S. Food and Drug Administration,
Federal Food, Drug, and Cosmetics Act (FDandC Act),
http://www.fda.gov/RegulatoryInformation/Legislation/FederalFoodDrugandCosmeticActFDCAct/default.htm

FDA, U.S. Food and Drug Administration,
Good Manufacturing Practice (GMP) Guildelines/Inspections Checklist,
http://www.fda.gov/Cosmetics/GuidanceComplianceRegulatoryInformation/GoodManufacturingPracticeGMPGuidelinesInspectionChecklist/default.htm

FDA, U.S. Food and Drug Administration,
Guidance, Compliance and Regulatory Information,
http://www.fda.gov/Cosmetics/GuidanceComplianceRegulatoryInformation/default.htm

FDA, U.S. Food and Drug Administration,
Is It a Cosmetic, a Drug, or Both? (Or Is It Soap?),
http://www.fda.gov/Cosmetics/GuidanceComplianceRegulatoryInformation/ucm074201.htm

FDA, U.S. Food and Drug Administration,
Product and Ingredient Safety,
http://www.fda.gov/Cosmetics/ProductandIngredientSafety/default.htm

Health Canada,
List of Prohibited and Restricted Cosmetic Ingredients ("Hotlist"),
http://www.hc-sc.gc.ca/cps-spc/cosmet-person/indust/hot-list-critique/index-eng.php

Health Canada,
Cosmetics and Your Health,
http://www.hc-sc.gc.ca/hl-vs/iyh-vsv/prod/cosmet-eng.php

Health Canada,
Consumer Product Safety,
http://www.hc-sc.gc.ca/cps-spc/cosmet-person/indust/index-eng.php

Health Canada,
Cosmetics and Personal Care, For Consumers and For Industry and Professionals,
http://www.hc-sc.gc.ca/cps-spc/cosmet-person/index-eng.php

International Organization for Standardization,
http://www.iso.org/iso/home.html

Japan Ministry of Health, Labor and Welfare,
Standards for Cosmetics, No. 331 of 2000,
http://www.mhlw.go.jp/english/dl/cosmetics.pdf

Merriam-Webster Online Dictionary,
2011 Merriam-Webster, Incorporated,
http://www.merriam-webster.com

Lees, Mark PhD; Milady's Skin Care Reference Guide,
Milady Publishing Company, New York; 1994

Official Journal of the European Union,
Directive 2003/15/EC of the European Parliament and of the Council
of 27 February 2003, amending Council Directive 76/768/ECC on the
approximation of the laws of the Member States relating to cosmetic products,
11.3.2003, L 66/26
*http://eur-lex.europa.eu/LexUriServ/LexUriServ.do?uri=OJ:L:2003:066:0026:00
35:en:PDF*

PubMed.gov,
U.S. National library of Medicine, National Institute of Health,
http://www.ncbi.nlm.nih.gov/pubmed/

Regulatory Toxicology and Pharmacology,
Official Journal of the International Society for Regulatory Toxicology and
Pharmacology, Elsevier Science, Gio B. Gori, DSc, MPH, ATS

Science Dictionary,
Chemistry Terms and Definitions Listed Alphabetically, Science Dictionary -
Scientific Definitions 2003-2006,
http://www.sciencedictionary.org/chemistry/

The Center for Drug Evaluation and Research (CDER),
http://www.fda.gov/Drugs/default.htm

Tisserand, Robert.
Essential Oils in Soap: Interview with Kevin Dunn, June 25, 2011
http://roberttisserand.com/2011/06/essential-oils-in-soap-interviewwith-kevin-dunn/

U.S. Consumer Product Safety Commission,
Office of Compliance, Requirements under the Federal Hazardous Substances
Act: Labeling and Banning Requirements for Chemical and Other Hazardous
Substances, 15 U.S.C, 161 and 16 C.F.R. Part 1500,
http://www.cpsc.gov/BUSINFO/regsumfhsa.pdf

U.S. Consumer Product Safety Commission,
Office of Compliance, Requirements under the Poison Prevention Packaging
Act, 16 C.F.R. 1700,
http://www.cpsc.gov/BUSINFO/regsumpppa.pdf

Index

127